COVENT GARI

by John Richardson

ISBN 0 9503656 1 0

First published 1979
Printed in Great Britain by
Royston Press, Middlesex.
Typeset by Bow-Towning Ltd.

Published by
Historical Publications Ltd
54 Station Road
New Barnet, Herts.

COVENT GARDEN

by John Richardson

HISTORICAL PUBLICATIONS

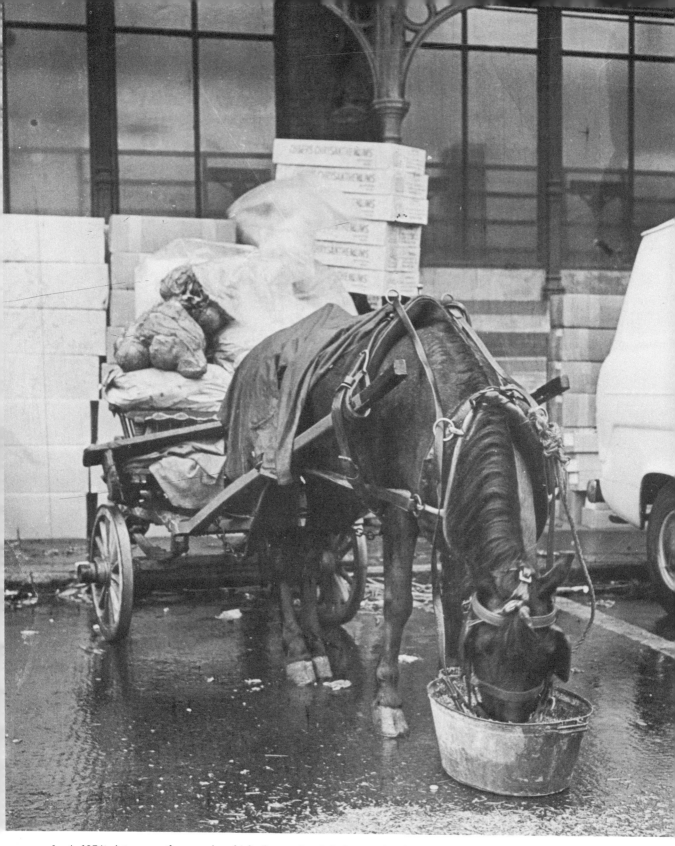

1. A 1974 picture — the year in which the market left Covent Garden.

Acknowledgements

The *Survey of London* series, now edited by Professor F.H.W. Sheppard, is a source which historical writers cannot ignore. In particular the sumptuous volume on *The Parish of St Paul, Covent Garden* (Volume 36) has been of great value in the research for this book and I not only acknowledge that freely, but also my admiration for the high level of scholarship it displays.

I have received help at various libraries, but in particular at Holborn Central Library (London Borough of Camden), the Greater London History Library at County Hall — arguably the most pleasant library building in London in which to work — and the Westminster Central Library. Mr Phillips of the Greater London Council Map and Print Collection and Miss Watson of the GLC Photographic Collection, have both given valuable assistance.

I am grateful also to representatives from Moss Bros, *The Lady,* J. Sainsbury Ltd, and Penhaligons Ltd for information on the history of their companies. Martin Coomes of the Covent Garden Community Association was also of great help.

The Illustrations

Cover illustration: Covent Garden Market, an aquatint by Thomas Rowlandson and A. Pugin.

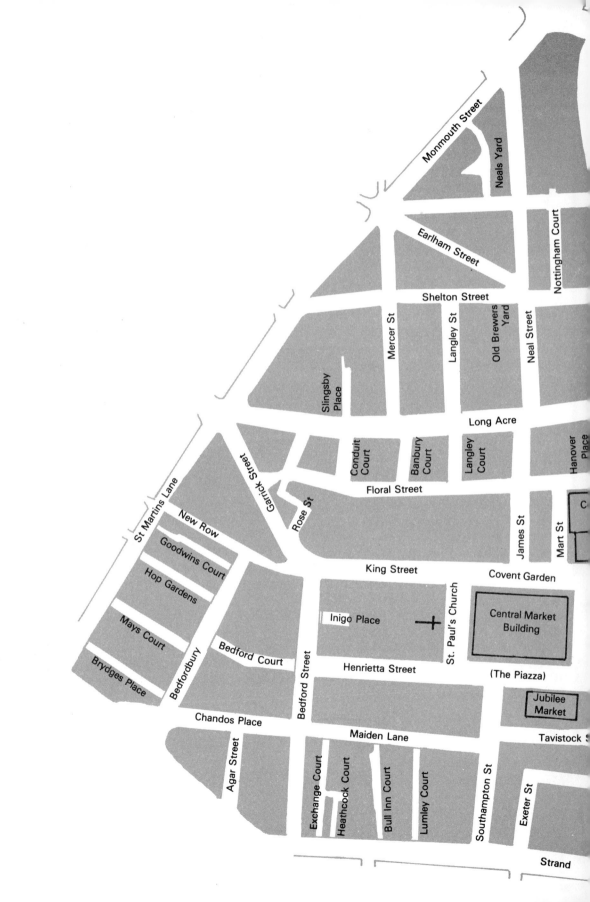

COVENT GARDEN

Based upon the Ordnance Survey
with the permission of
The Controller of Her Majesty's Stationery Office,
Crown Copyright Reserved

The Present

Covent Garden is in transition. The removal of the fruit and vegetable market in November 1974 to its new home at Nine Elms, left approximately 15 acres vacant and the planners, public and residents at odds with each other as to their future. To the planners it meant, taking in the surrounding area, a unique opportunity to design and significantly plan a very large part of central London. The residents who cared for such matters had plans for better residential areas augmented by shops, social amenities, small businesses and workshops, using the old buildings vacated.

In the event the battle was settled by the public's suspicion of grand schemes and the inability of the government and local authorities to afford one. The Minister for the Environment confused things even more by strategically listing so many buildings to be retained, that a grand plan was impossible to implement anyway. What is emerging now, since a second planning document, is a combination of show-piece renovation, such as the main market buildings, large housing schemes, such as the ones in Long Acre and Endell Street, office blocks such as the ones in Long Acre and James Street, and renovation and use by small businesses of the vacated shops and warehouses.

If there is an overall direction to the area's new life, it is not particularly apparent, except that it is becoming uncomfortably 'smart', and it is arguable that we are best off without one. After all, it was as recently as 1968, when certainly the *public* was generally aware of the pitfalls of large-scale development, that the planners proposed to demolish approximately 50% of the area — a scale of destruction now unthinkable. Overall directions can be dangerous things.

Conversely, the area is too important to be left to its own devices. It could, too easily, become an adjunct of Soho, or else an enormous craft workshop, a residential area of expensive and local authority housing, or an area without a stamp of identity. It could become too sleazy or too smart.

The area, however, has an historic base of activity, aside from the market, which can be built upon. It has been for 200 years, a home for publishers, printers, theatres, restaurants, pubs and specialised businesses. It is becoming rapidly the centre of London's crafts; it is adding galleries and small-scale, inexpensive entertainment. It has also a stock of the most inadequate housing in central London.

Above all, it seems to have a working and residential population that cares very much about its future — an unusual juxtaposition of concern and opportunity in London. The careful studies which highlighted the need for off-street parking, vehicular corridors , and linked pedestrian spaces seem entirely irrelevant to this commitment. People, on the whole, do not want tidiness, logistical convenience or even cleanliness particularly. They want unexpected things, unobtrusive courtyards, street life, the facility to open ostensibly uneconomic businesses and the harmony and satisfaction that comes from a genuine mixing of people and outlooks.

Covent Garden is not a collection of vistas. The 1968 Plan made great play of its objective method of isolating 'sequences of visual experience', (a phrase to deaden the senses), and found not many at all. In so doing, it ignored, because it chose to, the historical development of the area, which was that of piece-meal rebuilding when it became absolutely necessary within a congested street plan. Indifferent buildings stand next to gems, working places overshadow houses. It is an assortment of individual buildings from different periods requiring subjective admiration and a sense and knowledge of the past.

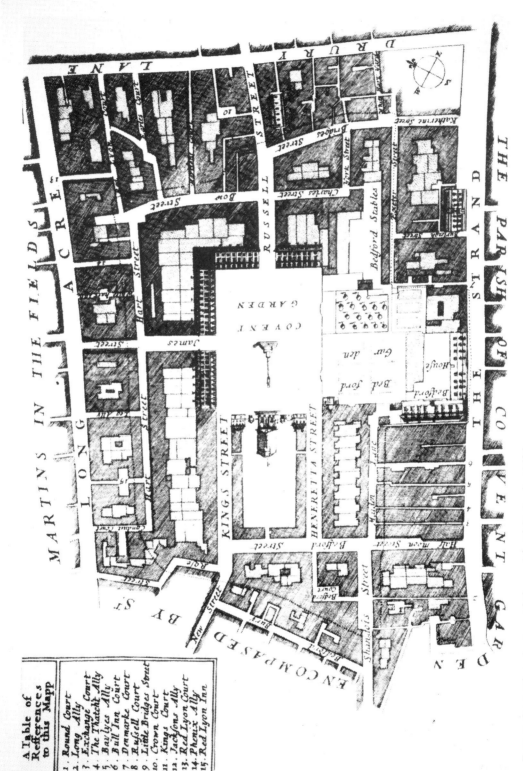

A Table of
References
to this Mapp

1. Round Court
2. Long Ally
3. Exchange Court
4. The Thatcht Ally
5. Baylyes Ally
6. Bull Inn Court
7. Denmarke Court
8. Rysell Court
9. Little Bridges Street
10. Crown Court
11. Kings Court
12. Jacksons Ally
13. Red Lyon Court
14. Phœnix Ally
15. Red Lyon Inn

3. *Extract from Blome's map of the parish of St Paul, c1686.*

General History

Early Days

Covent Garden derives its name from a market garden here belonging to the Benedictine Convent of St Peter's, Westminster in the middle ages. Most of the inner part of north London at that time was held by the church and monasteries; the seizure, by Henry VIII, of church lands in the 16th century is one of the most crucial factors in the development of London.

The market garden was usually leased out to individuals to make what profit they could from its produce. The Convent also held 7 acres to the north called Long Acre and two pieces of land called Friars Pyes, fronting the Strand, where Southampton Street is today.

In 1536 the Convent exchanged their garden and Long Acre — one suspects they were obliged to do so — with Henry VIII, for the Priory of Hurley in Berkshire, an estate the King had already seized from the church anyway. Friars Pyes were also taken by the Crown four years later when Westminster Abbey was suppressed.

By 1552 these pieces of land had come into the possession of John Russell, the first Earl of Bedford. Thus began a landlord and tenant relationship that was to last for nearly 400 years.

The Bedford family, shown much favour by successive monarchs, eventually owned many estates in the country and London. To this day, they still own a large part of Bloomsbury, immediately north of Covent Garden. From them and their country seats London derives street names such as Tavistock, Russell, Chenies, Woburn, Crowndale, Eversholt, Howland, Chandos and Malet.

John Russell lived on the south side of the Strand — the highway from the City to the Palace of Westminster, along which noblemen had erected their large houses on space not available in the crowded City. Russell did not develop the Covent Garden estate but merely let it out for pasture or horticulture. His great-grandson Edward, the third Earl, built for himself a house roughly on the site of Southampton Street, on sloping ground which would have given him a view of the Thames. This house was demolished in 1706 as the then Duke of Bedford preferred to live in Bloomsbury.

By 1613, the third Earl had built a brick wall round the convent garden, enclosing an area of about 20 acres. Outside this wall, various building schemes, such as the development of Long Acre, had begun. It was within this wall that the fourth Earl set about what was to be the first major piece of town planning in London, with a spaciousness and opulence previously unknown. The present-day grid of wide streets, surrounded by the more congested ones, shows clearly the plan inside the wall. It was an instant success.

The First Development

Francis, the fourth Earl, reputed to be greedy, uncultured and shunned by Court society, was also the first great speculative builder in London. He was responsible, too, for the draining of the Fens and the rebuilding of Woburn Abbey. He was fortunate, in Covent Garden, in having a king, Charles I, who was keen to have his capital city ornamented outside the City walls. He had thrust upon him too, by the Crown, its own Surveyor-of-the-King's Works as architect, Inigo Jones.

Jones introduced Renaissance architecture into England, adapting Italian ideas, especially those of Palladio. He built the Queen's House at Greenwich and the Banqueting House in Whitehall. To him we probably owe the concept of the Covent Garden scheme and its Piazza, and certainly to him the design of St Paul's Church.

The warrant and licence obtained by the Earl from the Crown to build Covent Garden, stated that he was to build 'houses and buildings fit for the habitaçons of Gentlemen and men of ability'. The Earl showed his gratitude by naming some of the main streets in honour of the Royal family. King Street commemorates Charles I, James Street his son (later James II), Henrietta Street his Queen, and Charles Street (later Wellington Street) his son, later Charles II.

The Piazza, upon which the market developed, and the Church, were the centrepieces around which the wide streets, (for those days), radiated. Oddly enough little attempt was made to provide adequate access into this arrangement from the surrounding high roads. This was remedied much later when the rest of the old wall came down and when James Street was widened at Long Acre and Southampton and Garrick Streets built.

4. *View of the Piazza c1717-28, looking north. Engraved by Sutton Nicholls.*

The layout of the scheme is shown in illustration 3, which depicts Bedford House fronting the Strand.

The scheme was financed by the Earl and a large number of speculators to whom he granted leases. The Earl paid for the scheme's initial outlay, the underground foundation vaults, some houses on the Piazza, and the Church. Speculators would have had to build to minimum standards and within a style, for the uniformity of houses here was remarked upon.

The Piazza itself was an innovation in London — an open square for exercise and social meetings. On three sides was a total of seventeen houses, built between 1633 and 1637, much in the style of the present Bedford Chambers on the north side, which were erected in 1879, modelled on the old buildings. The original houses were four-storey with the upper floors extending over the covered walk. All this is now lost, but some idea of what it looked like can be had from illustrations 4 and 5. Market stalls are shown at the south end near the pillar. The Church remains, eventually to lose its prominence when hemmed in by market buildings. In these engravings can be seen the newly-built No 43 King Street, just north of the Church facing towards the square, built in place of the earlier end house. This is still here. To the south were also some houses, not so grand, backing on to the gardens of Bedford House.

The economic life of Covent Garden in the 18th century had four main supports — the market, carriage making, the theatres and small businesses.

The growth of the market was necessary to feed an expanding London. In turn, this provided employment for residents and transients, but the main profits were scooped by the Bedford family in the form of market tolls from the dealers who brought their produce here.

The carriage-making trade settled in Long Acre; it reached its peak in the mid 19th century,only to collapse with the advent of the car. All the poorer streets around had premises housing specialists working on upholstery, lace trimmings, riding equipment, coach lamps and other fittings. Compared with the market, it provided a real economic support.

The theatres encouraged allied activities such as costumiers, but their real influence was felt in the number of inns and coffee-houses. The heyday of the coffee-houses was the 18th century and this reflects the social attitude of that day. The most famous artists and writers were then public figures in a more personal sense. There they were, in the flesh, available for conversation and greetings. They were not under the pressure of today's illustrious names who are forced to seek the seclusion of expensive restaurants, only to appear publicly, but in isolation, on our television screens.

The number of small, craft businesses in Covent Garden was vast and the variety probably unique in London's history. This element exists today.

The inner Covent Garden area is a parish on its own — St Paul's. To the west and south is the parish of St Martin's-in-the-Fields and to the north and east, St Giles-in-the-Fields. These areas too, if not built upon already, were being developed at the same time, but to a meaner standard. In particular, the St Giles part quickly degenerated to provide an early example of London's tendency to have squalor and opulence in adjacent streets.

Seven Dials, consisting of seven roads radiating from a central column constructed at the end of the 17th century, Bedfordbury and its adjacent courts, Drury Lane, with its squalid surroundings, all hemmed in a previously fashionable area that was itself socially complicated by the growth of the market. That the central area did not become totally beyond recall is due to its single ownership by the Bedford family. The principal streets maintained enough status for regeneration in the 19th century to be financially possible.

Nowadays, the positioning of one or two theatres within a mainly residential area would be welcomed as enriching, or even socially enhancing, a neighbourhood. This is because the theatre is now respectable. In the 17th and 18th centuries theatres acquired the cachet of a modern strip club or massage parlour. Together with the many inns and private drinking houses, they were the embodiment of the loose-living required and necessary in any capital city in the world.

This social factor in Covent Garden came to its peak in the 18th century, when the seemingly inseparable evils of poverty and drunkenness

5. *View of the Piazza looking north, in c1746. From a drawing by J. Maurer.*

reached proportions unimaginable today. Soho today is tawdry, but really quite mild when compared to the violence, social irresponsibility and prostitution present in Covent Garden in the 18th century. Foreign visitors were taken aback by the youth of the girls who accosted them. A social attitude which tolerated the King having a former fruit-seller as a mistress, or the normality of men spending several evenings a week in brothels, gathered its own momentum, so that the human debris became too much for the primitive parish organisations to cope with. Even putting aside this aspect of life, the living conditions of the poor and exploited were such that disease could run unchecked and only the cheap, and quite often poisonous, drink could bring solace.

The problems did not go away of their own accord — they stayed in various degrees for at least 200 years. Their concentration in Covent Garden abated simply because social life in London shifted, but definite inroads and improvements were made by the late 19th century reformers.

What must have been obvious social distress in Covent Garden, is now drawn, in retrospective histories, almost as a back-drop to the glamour of the theatres and the coffee houses. In the same way as names like Irving, Kean and Garrick roll off the tongues as giants in the theatre, (and one suspects that by today's standards they were pretty awful actors), we tend to be uncritical or unaware of the real nature of life at that period. Women, in particular, were exploited, and not just for pleasure. They worked hard in the market and carried enormous loads to and from the market gardens in outer London. They were the cheap labour which kept the better houses going.

Covent Garden and its surroundings, in short, contained then some of the worst social conditions London has ever known.

The 19th century brought many changes and much new building. Most of the streets in the area are 19th century, as are the market buildings. Warehousing became important as the market grew and the mean streets adjacent to Seven Dials became full of them.

New concentrations of business emerged — in particular, publishing and printing. Catherine, Tavistock and Wellington Streets were concerned principally with newspapers and magazines. Bedford and Henrietta Streets housed publishers. Long Acre and nearby became the home of printers. Hotels flourished and at one time almost the whole of the Piazza was taken over by them until they moved north, mainly to Bloomsbury, when the railways came to Euston Road.

Social reform was gathering force. Bedfordbury and the Parker Street area were drastically altered by the Peabody Trust, and small mission halls and schools abounded. In Bow Street, the magistrates' court was built on its present site, the alleyways made hygienic and presentable and the whole area, especially the southern end of Drury Lane, made more impersonal. Endell Street, with its baths, workhouse, school and hospital, had a

6. *St Paul's Church, by Hollar.*

significant influence on the area.

The two theatres were no longer novelties or special in London. Once their performing monopolies had been revoked, theatres were common and cultural life moved abruptly westwards. The social life surrounding them moved out as well, leaving Covent Garden to its own devices.

There has been little new building in Covent Garden in the 20th century and the boom between the wars hardly affected it. Businesses and people were too busy moving out to the suburbs. Possibly redevelopment might have occurred had the landowning dominance of the Bedfords not been a factor, for certainly the area badly needed renovation.

Instead, a gradual deterioration set in. The Bedfords were more anxious to sell than to improve. The market traders, no respecters of architectural niceties, spoilt many of the finer buildings, especially in King Street, and a period came when everything was in a vacuum. It was obvious that the market would have to move and possibly it would have done much earlier, but for the two world wars. Ironically, we can be grateful that these probably saved what is Covent Garden today, because there would have been scant enthusiasm for conservation in the 1930s when a brave new world seemed as desirable and imminent as in the 1950s. Demolition would have been the trend and one has only to look at other parts of London to envisage the style of rebuilding.

The Bedfords eventually sold out to the Beechams without regret, except that the Duke found he had unwittingly included his private box at Covent Garden in the sale. The new owners proceeded to sell most of the property except for the market proper.

After the last war there was another period of uncertainty. A new market elsewhere was certain to come and its imminence blighted the area to an extent which persuaded the planners that not much was worth saving. However, that was a period when houses were regarded as having a useful life of only sixty years and building societies had no confidence in such properties. Those were heady, frontier days, uncomplicated by nostalgia, unworried by the lack of craftsmanship in our new environments.

As the market moved out, small businesses moved in, attracted by the then low rents and the spaces — unusual in central London. There was a dilemma here for the authorities: the properties could not be left vacant for years — the deterioration would affect the better premises adversely, but the new tenants, however short their leases, would eventually claim public sympathy as sitting, and quite often socially useful, tenants.

In the event conservation caught up with the right moment.

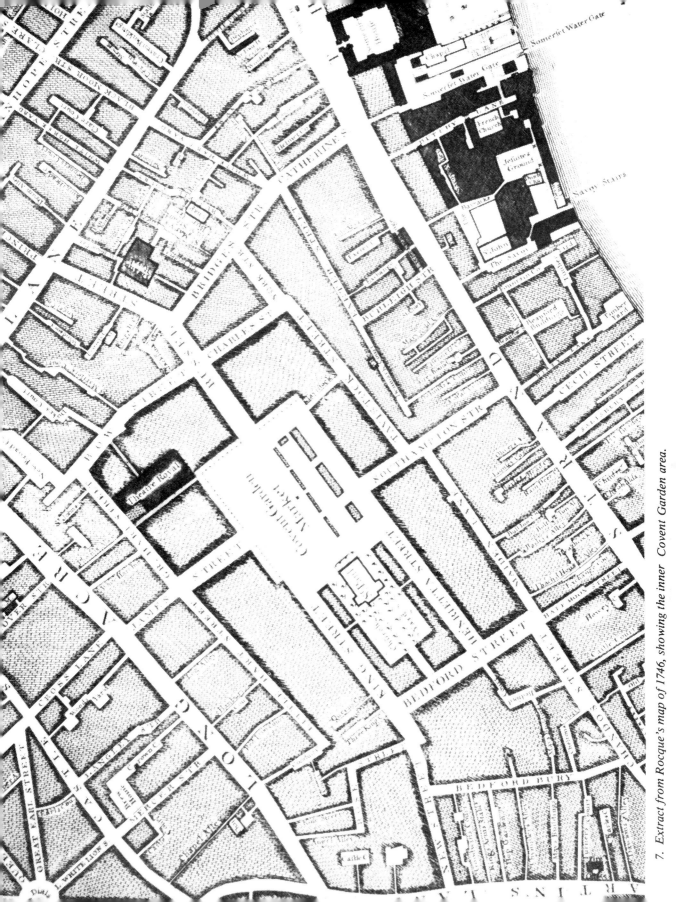

7. Extract from Rocque's map of 1746, showing the inner Covent Garden area.

The Replanning of Covent Garden

The publication, in 1968, of *'Covent Garden's Moving'*, a document which laid down proposals for the redevelopment of Covent Garden and areas adjacent, produced an inevitable outcry. The Greater London Council and their associates in a consortium, Westminster and Camden councils, suggested the demolition of about half the area and the introduction of major roads. A public enquiry was begun in 1971 and at last in 1974 the planners were told to think again, this time disciplined by a much larger number of buildings listed for retention.

Clearly, no wholesale scheme could now be envisaged and subsequent proposals meet most conservationists' demands. This does not mean that the battle to keep Covent Garden roughly in its old form is won — politics and planners are not that constant — but it is true to say that public opinion, which won the first round, is now more organised to take the contest.

In theory development will involve, and has done for some years, close consultation with the local residents through an organisation referred to as the Forum, on which various categories of residents have representation. However, the real test of this exercise in democracy will come in the next few years, as Covent Garden becomes the most attractive place in central London in which to work and live. For all the sympathetic planning documents, the forces of commercial interests will eventually militate against not only the needs of the residents, but the pleasure the visitor derives from its present harmony.

It is, perhaps, unfair with the newer plan being implemented, to repeat again some of the concepts in the 1968 document. But in trying to assess what is wanted for the area now, it is worth reminding ourselves of a paragraph in the introduction to the 1968 Plan, which pressed for an international conference centre and more major hotels to be built here. Taken with the proposals for major roads, this shows that the planners had an entirely different view of the area's role to the one which they are now obliged to propound. It was a concept of largeness, all neatly softened by other plans to ease the residents' lot.

The latest plan, which draws heavily upon the wishes of the residents, essentially thinks small. Generally it is a negative plan and acceptable because of this. It prohibits certain kinds of development and use, it retains most buildings, it backs down on the proposal to carve out a 3 acre open space and settles instead for a series of smaller open spaces totalling 3 acres, and it seeks the modernisation of the sub-standard housing.

To offset this apparent about-face it is now becoming apparent that commercial interests are being allowed to play a harmful part in the area's future. Leases of shops and warehouses owned by the GLC are apparently being let to the highest bidder and, provided that the business proposed does not infringe wide guide-lines, it will get the lease. Hence, Covent Garden is becoming full of expensive shops and wine-bars which will need the tourists to pay their rents. It is assumed, by the leasing authority, that the maximum financial return must be obtained from buildings. In other words, social desirability is not governing the choices made.

This trend will eventually diminish the intrinsic charm of Covent Garden. When the London Transport Museum and the National Theatre Museum open and nearly half a million visitors come, the pressure to make Covent Garden even more profitable will squeeze out the small shops and businesses — at least the ones which are useful to the working and living population. The tourist, as other parts of London — especially Chelsea — will verify, is a dubious blessing.

The large-scale developments under way or proposed at the time of writing are:

The Flower Market Building will house the London Transport Museum on its transfer from Syon Park. This is a collection of buses, trams and trains expected to attract between 300,000 and 400,000 visitors annually, many of them in coach parties.

Also in this building, will be the National Theatre Museum, newly established from material in the Victoria and Albert Museum and in private collections. It will be the major museum of theatrical history in this country.

The central market building will become mainly shops, with some studios and workshops and, surrounded by a paved, traffic free Piazza, will be the showpiece of Covent Garden.

8. *The central market building being renovated in May 1979.*

The Jubilee Market on the south side of the Piazza is still in contention. At present there is a covered market and a sports hall, but the planners argue, with some justification, that this building spoils the symmetry of the square and should be rebuilt to achieve an architectural harmony never achieved before. The new building will have an arcaded pedestrian walk. The Jubilee Hall, then, is the only main market building likely to go.

In Long Acre one of the two vacant sites will mainly be for housing, and the other for offices.

Camden Council has demolished Dudley House, the old workhouse and hostel at the north of Endell Street, and is building homes, a community hall, other welfare facilities and shops.

The Peabody Trust is to demolish its blocks in Bedfordbury and erect new flats with a greater emphasis on family units.

The Royal Opera House is to build an extension to its south and west to house a second auditorium, the Royal Ballet School and the London Opera Centre. This will form part of the office development in James Street.

Other developments are small-scale.

What is referred to as the Comyn Ching Triangle, which sounds like a sinister Chinese organisation, but is really the premises of an ironmongery firm at Seven Dials, is to be partly rebuilt and partly renovated.

The Earlham Street Warehouse is to be rehabilitated to include homes on the fifth and a new sixth floor.

A street market is to be introduced into Drury Lane and Parker Street and encouragement generally given to make the northern part of Drury Lane a good, local shopping centre.

Housing will be introduced into what are basically industrial or commercial pockets such as Neals Yard, Matthews Yard, Hanover Place and Bedford Chambers.

Attractive as the market trade was, it had a serious effect on the architecture and condition of the many beautiful buildings in the area — the illustration of 43 King Street (No 83) shows what did happen to one of the most important houses. The Plan and the mounting appreciation of what is here in Covent Garden, will ensure that the buildings are renovated well, so that Covent Garden will once again, as in the 17th century, be a place to gaze at and admire.

9. *Extract from Rocque's map of 1746, showing the outer Covent Garden area and, to the north, the Bedford possession of Bloomsbury.*

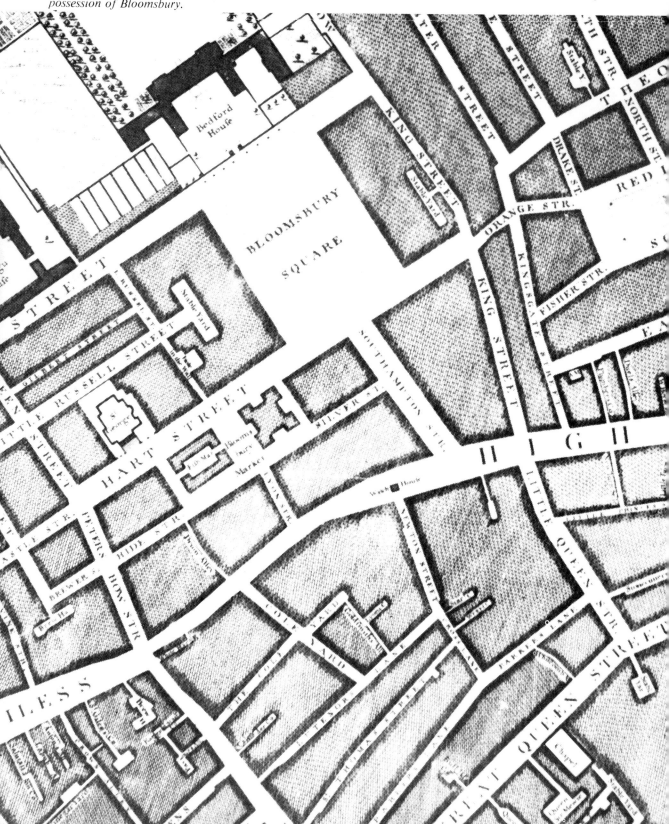

The Streets

AGAR STREET

Agar Street was a narrow passage called Long Alley in the 17th century, connecting Chandos Place to the Strand. It was rebuilt c1738 as Castle Court and then in 1830, Agar Street was built on the line to a wider measure as part of the general road improvements around the Trafalgar Square area. It derives its name from George Agar Ellis, Chief Commissioner of Woods and Forests, oddly enough, the Government department responsible for development in the area.

It is dominated on its west by the 1830s Charing Cross Hospital (a listed building by Decimus Burton), now a refuge for down and outs, and on the east by the side of the Civil Service Stores and the flank wall of the long empty Rhodesia House. This latter building pays no rates, because it would be illegal to accept them, and receives, judging by the look of the outside, no maintenance. Its stone figures of lithe Empire builders, sculpted by Jacob Epstein, on the side of the building, are as worn as the negotiators trying to achieve a settlement for that unhappy country.

ARNE STREET

Half of Arne Street is demolished. The most interesting features in the road are the hoardings around the redevelopment with their emphasis on philosophical statement — at least they were there at the time of writing.

Thomas Arne (1710-78), composer, was born in King Street, Covent Garden, son of an upholsterer. He is remembered chiefly for composing *Rule Britannia* but the appendage of his name in 1911 to this tiny street, (once called Dirty Lane), perhaps redresses that rather grand image. (*Illustration 10*)

BANBURY COURT

This Court, running between Floral Street and Long Acre, is named after of the Earl of Banbury who lived in Long Acre. His house was demolished in 1699 and the Court, presumably, formed at that time.

BEDFORD COURT

Bedford Court is not what it was. It now consists

10. *Thomas Arne, from a drawing by F. Bartolozzi.*

of the sides of buildings and it goes now in a new direction. Originally it had shops, including two coffee-houses, and was described as being well-inhabited. When it was laid out in the 1630s it went from Bedford Street, which it still does, and then opened south into Chandos Place. This route was added to in 1881 by allowing it to go west through the Peabody Estate, then being built, to Bedfordbury. In 1903, when the Charing Cross Hospital Medical School was being expanded, its southern entrance was closed.

BEDFORD STREET

Originally it was planned that Bedford Street, pursuing a slightly different line, should lead out to the Strand in full width. The Earl of Bedford, however, was unable to buy the necessary land facing the Strand and had to position Bedford Street so that, at least, there was access through what was known as Half Moon Street, an existing narrow alley originally part of the back courtyard of the Half Moon Inn on the Strand. This explains why Bedford Street is much narrower today at its southern end.

Laid out in 1631 and completed within nine years, it became shops with residents above by the end of the century. One of its first buildings was

11. *Demolition of the corner of Bedford Street and Chandos Street before the Civil Service Store was built.*

on the west side facing Henrietta Street, called the Musaeum Minervae, a short-lived school for the sons of noblemen and gentlemen established by Sir Francis Kynaston, a courtier of Charles I. According to a contemporary report he had to resign as Cupbearer to the King because he trembled so much from nervousness. One professor at the school was responsible for teaching Latin, Greek, Hebrew, Spanish, French, Italian and German. The future kings, Charles II and James II, came to watch a masque performed here.

At about the same place lived Thomas Sheridan, the father of the dramatist Richard Brinsley Sheridan. One day, a visitor called to find Sheridan senior expecting a visit from Dr Johnson. Sheridan said to his guest "Take out your opera-glass, Johnson is coming; you may know him by his gait." The visitor records: "I perceived him at a good distance, working along with a peculiar solemnity of deportment and an awkward sort of measured step. At that time the

broad flagging at each side of the streets was not universally adopted, and stone posts were in fashion to prevent the annoyance of carriages. Upon every post, as he passed along, I could observe he deliberately laid his hand; but missing one of them, when he had got at some distance, he seemed suddenly to recollect himself, and immediately returning back, carefully performed the accustomed ceremony, and resumed his former course, not omitting one till he gained the crossing."

In the 19th century this street was dominated by publishing houses, as was Henrietta Street.

West Side
Nos 4/6

The Civil Service Store was built in 1877, the architects Lockwood and Mawson. The Civil Service Supply Association began in 1864, when some Post Office clerks in the City jointly bought a chest of tea and thereby made substantial savings on their individual shares. This led to

12. The Civil Service Store, Bedford Street frontage.

purchases of different commodities and eventually they formed themselves into the Post Office Supply Association. The service was gradually extended to other members of the Civil Service; staff had to pay 2/6d (12½p) per year for the privilege. In 1927 the Association went public and now has no link with the Civil Service.

The building, in red brick and terra cotta, is a combination of Victorian and Renaissance. *(Illustration 12)*

Nos 10/13

Aldine House has recently been vacated by the publishing firm of J.M. Dent. What the proprietor wanted, and thought he had, was a mixture of Elizabethan and Queen Anne and one can only conclude that the architect, E. Keynes Purchase, was very good at persuading his client that this essentially Edwardian building had the characteristics Dent was after.

Dent was born in 1849, the son of a house-painter and went to elementary school in Darlington. He became a bookbinder, came to London for work when he was 22 and opened his own bookbinding business in Hoxton five years later. His second premises were burnt down and with the insurance money he built a much larger business, branching out into publishing cheap editions in 1888. By the early 1890s he was established as a publisher.

Dents moved to 29/30 Bedford Street in 1898 (earlier the home of Macmillans), and it was here that he planned the series that was to make his reputation and fortune. He intended a cheap edition library of the world's greatest literature, a total of 1000 volumes. In the first twelve months, with Ernest Rhys as his literary editor, he published 153 titles under the name of the *Everyman Library*.

13. The headquarters of The Lady magazine, Nos 39/40 Bedford Street.

14. Nos 14-16 Bedford Street.

Frank Swinnerton, who worked for Dent, recalls in *The Bookman's London* that Dent was so silvery that many strangers mistook him for a saint. However, he had an unusually violent temper, he never praised, and paid very poorly. He frightened everybody who worked for him and, predictably, didn't seem to know why employees left him so rapidly.

Aldine House was opened in 1911.

Nos 14/16

These three houses were erected in 1863. The first occupants of No 14 were Wilkinson, Howlett and Matthews, solicitors. Their successors Wilkinson, Howlett and Durham were there until recently.

No 15 has been, since 1865, the premises of Frederick Warne, publishers, but at other times has housed Butterworths and Eyre & Spottiswoode, also publishers. Warnes in addition took premises in Bedford Court around the corner.

No 16 was an early home (until 1872) of Alexander Macmillan, one of the founders of Macmillan & Co, publishers. He then moved across the road to 29/30.

The architecture of these three buildings is attributed to S.S. Teulon but the style is not his usual one. *(Illustration 14)*

Nos 17/19

This post office and the sorting office at the rear were erected in 1884. Pevsner thinks the architect was E.G. Rivers, but the *Survey of London* suggests James Williams might have been.

Nos 21/26

The rest of this side of the street is dominated by Moss Brothers, the famous tailors, whose premises also stretch round the corner into King Street.

The founder of the firm, Moses Moses, opened a shop in Bedford Street (No 25) in 1860. He and his sons opened a similar shop in King Street in 1881, with a lacemakers occupying the corner building between them. Moss Bros. acquired the whole site in 1920.

The start of their celebrated hire business is recounted in a story kindly supplied by Moss Bros. In 1897 Alfred Moss, who was one of the Moss brothers, had a friend called Charles Pond, a stockbroker. In his heyday Charles Pond was

15. Moss Brothers, outfitters, in an early shop.

much in demand for weekend house parties because he loved to entertain people and was a talented amateur actor. When he fell on hard times he was still invited, but it was made clear to him that he was expected to sing for his supper. He came to see Alfred Moss one day and said to him that he had an invitation to a weekend party, but he had been obliged to pawn his dress clothes and could not afford to redeem the pledge. Alfred Moss lent him a tail suit and Charles Pond kept returning it to Alfred with the same story and request. In the end Alfred asked Charles to pay something towards the loan and a fee of 7/6d. (37½p) per hire was agreed. The news of this transaction became known in theatrical circles and thenceforth Moss Bros. were in the hire business. *(Illustration 15)*

East Side
No 27
Together with No 16 King Street, this corner site is the headquarters of the Communist Party of Great Britain. It was erected in 1862 for John Moseley, plane and tool manufacturer and by the 1880s it was the headquarters of the Green Room Club, a theatrical club now in Adam Street, south of the Strand. It has been surrounded on the ground floor by a supposedly attack-proof fascia of appalling dreariness.

Nos 28/30
This is a handsome, 1873, Italianate building. Macmillans the publishers came here when it was built, then Dents (see Nos 10/13). It has since been used by publishers, including Debretts and Odhams and, more recently, by Richard Seifert the architect of the tower blocks Centre Point and Space House which loom over the area.

Nos 39/40

The Lady magazine, occupiers of this building, was launched in 1885 by Thomas Gibson Bowles, already the proprietor and editor of *Vanity Fair*. The week of the first edition was a sad one for Bowles: his step-mother, to whom he was devoted, died and his closest friend was killed at the fall of Khartoum. Bowles had started *Vanity Fair,* then primarily a satirical paper, at the age of 25 with £200 in his pocket. It was published, together with *The Lady* from 12 Tavistock Street.

The Lady was not the first women's magazine, but it was in a virtually untapped market. Its publication was advertised and provoked C.L. Dodgson (Lewis Carroll) to object to the wording of the advertisement, in particular the phrase "To look beautiful is one of the first duties of a lady." The first edition sold 2361 copies (circulation is now 80,000) and lost £209. The paper did not break even until 1886. On its staff once, before she became famous with *Cold Comfort Farm,* was the authoress Stella Gibbons.

The move to 39/40 Bedford Street was made in 1881, the printing presses being installed in the basement. These premises, rebuilt in 1861, had previously been used by metal manufacturers.

The rest of Bedford Street, down to the Strand, was once Half Moon Street, It is now dominated by the shop fronts and whatever architectural merit there was has disappeared. No 45, for example, used to be a pub called The Green Man, but has now had installed down its front some extraordinary 1930s features, to sit uneasily upon the restaurant. The history of this part of the street is one of refreshment rooms and family shops, although there was a hotel at No 46 in the 1950-60s.

BEDFORDBURY

The origins of this street name are obscure. The Bedford part is understandable but the 'bury' part, meaning a fortified place, seems unlikely. Perhaps it is just a fanciful name. The street was formerly the central roadway through a number of insanitary alleyways such as May's Buildings, Chymister's Alley, Turner's Court and Hop Gardens etc. It was largely changed when the Peabody Estate was built in 1881. George Peabody was an American philanthropist (1795-1869), whose ancestors emigrated from Leicester to America in 1635. After making a fortune from stores, Peabody came back to England and set up business as a banker.

The Peabody Trust buildings are due for demolition.

Nos 23/24, now a restaurant, are very attractive 18th century buildings, giving onto Goodwin's Court. No 24 has two mansard storeys.

The Lemon Tree pub is c1880, but there was an inn of that name here much earlier — indeed in 1840 there were six pubs in this street.

BETTERTON STREET

This street was substantially built in the 19th century on the line of the 18th century Brownlow Street. This area had become very undesirable by the 19th century; even in the 1750s this must have applied, as there was a passageway off called Dirty Lane.

The most impressive building here is No 24, Brownlow House, an 18th century house with a fine doorcase. Its name derives from Sir James Brownlow who owned Lennox House near Drury Lane — a building demolished c1682.

The present street name dates from 1877. Thomas Betterton (1635-1710) was the leading actor of his day. He made his first appearance at the Cockpit Theatre in Drury Lane and he is credited with having introduced moving scenery into this country to replace the hanging tapestries then in common use.

BOW STREET

It is supposed that Bow Street derives its name from its contours which are slightly curved, but not excessively so. It did not open into Long Acre until 1793 and in 1835, when Wellington Street was formed, it became a throughway to the Strand.

Bow Street was laid out in the 1630s with the usual mixture of good-class housing and shops, but its character changed considerably in the 18th century. Covent Garden Theatre was built in 1732, a small magistrate's court was opened in 1740 just south of the Theatre on the same side of the road, and the parish opened a poorhouse here in 1723. Furthermore, Will's Coffee House, on the corner with Russell Street, was famous by the 1690s due to Dryden's patronage. At the end of the 18th century the character of the street was set as one of semi-public buildings.

In the 19th century the trend was continued. A new police station was built in 1832 at Nos 33/34 (the site of the new Telephone Exchange), and the present Magistrates' Court and Police Station were erected in 1880. The Opera House was rebuilt after a fire in 1856 and the Floral Hall was opened in 1860, to complete the picture, until the new Telephone Exchange was built in 1967.

The street has had a number of famous residents. The Fieldings are its best known. Robert Harley, 1st Earl of Oxford, was born here in 1661 — the collection of books and manuscripts owned by him and his son was one of the main foundations of the British Museum Library. Another library name lived here — Dr John Radcliffe (1650-1714), whose patients included William III and Queen Anne, left a sum of money which helped to found the Bodleian Library at Oxford.

Grinling Gibbons, the carver, was here in the last quarter of the 17th century, Charles Macklin, the actor, (from whom Macklin Street is named), was here 1743-8, and William Wycherley, the dramatist, lodged in Bow Street in 1715.

West Side
No 1

This is the corner building with Russell Street and is the site of one of the best-known coffee houses — Will's. It was opened in 1671 by William Urwin from whom it took its name. Coffee houses were a phenomenon of the late 17th and early 18th century London social life. One nowadays tends to yawn at the rambling descriptions of who met who at whichever establishment and the significance which is attached to the social life in them. Certainly there is a nauseating, breathless awe in the reverence which some historical writers attach to the presence in these establishments of famous artists. Also, our own social life nowadays is spread over a much wider spectrum of meeting places and it is difficult to appreciate the importance of coffee houses as focal points.

John Dryden, the poet, made Will's famous by his extended patronage and here he held court with his reserved position by the fire or by the window, depending upon the season. Because he was here less illustrious artists of the day came to

16. John Dryden.

listen to or stare at him. Its clientèle also included Pope, Steele and Addison, but Dryden was the magnet and even Pepys came to see him here. *(Illustration 16)*

By 1743 it was called Chapman's Coffee House and probably went out of business soon after. According to street directories, No 1 was a pub called The Grapes until the 2nd World War.

Site of No 4

This site is now covered by market buildings, but it ranks as one of the most famous addresses in the history of English justice. In 1740 Thomas De Veil, a Middlesex magistrate, (this area was part of the County of Middlesex then), acquired the house and used it as a magistrate's office. Soon after he died Henry Fielding, who had just married his dead wife's maid, took over the house and used it also while he was a Justice of the Peace. This was in 1747.

Fielding had led the proverbial dissipated youth. He wrote plays now ignored, including one that drew a laugh from Swift who, it is said, smiled only twice in his life. In 1735 Fielding owned a theatre in the Haymarket. By 1740 he had enlarged his preoccupations and was called to the Bar. He was made a Justice of the Peace, wrote books on the containment of crime and

17. *No 4 Bow Street — the first magistrate's court. From a watercolour by J. Winston.*

18. *Sir John Fielding's court at work, at No 4 Bow Street.*

19. *The Magistrate's court in 1808. From an aquatint by Thomas Rowlandson and A. Pugin.*

during all this wrote the classic *'The History of Tom Jones'*. He found time also to edit the *Covent Garden Journal,* a popular newspaper of the day. He was, as every schoolboy knows, the originator of the 'Bow Street Runners', an early crime squad formed after his death in 1754. He was succeeded by his blind half-brother Sir John Fielding who consolidated the work of the Court and the police. In 1828 the 'Bow Street Runners' were superseded by Robert Peel's force of men called, among other, ruder, names, 'Peelers'. The present-day term for a policeman — 'Bobby' — derives from Sir Robert Peel. *(Illustrations 17, 18, 19 and 23)*

The Court continued here until the present buildings on the other side of the street were erected in 1880. The police side of the business had already moved in 1832.

Covent Garden Theatre

Covent Garden Theatre is now the national home for opera in this country, with a stage and auditorium considerably smaller than other major European opera houses possess.

The first theatre, designed by Edward Shepherd, opened in 1732. It was managed and built by John Richard, owner of one of the two Crown patents to run a theatre in London and Westminster (Drury Lane Theatre held the other one).

Before this first building burnt down in 1808 it had staged the first performance of *'She Stoops to Conquer'* in 1773 and had launched a famous (at the time) juvenile tragedian called Master Betty. Charles Macklin made his last appearance here as Shylock at the very advanced age of either 99 or 89, depending upon which birth date you accept.

20. The present Covent Garden Theatre and Floral Hall, both by E. M Barry, architect.

Towards the end of its life, the building was managed by the Kemble family and two of its members, John Philip and Sarah Siddons, appeared here.

Twenty three firemen were killed when the theatre burnt down. In addition some of Handel's original scores were lost. (*The Messiah* had been first performed in this country at Covent Garden in 1741).

The second building, by Robert Smirke, was opened in 1809. It was modelled on the Temple of Minerva on the Acropolis. Kemble, the manager, had to raise seat prices to help pay for it and his action provoked riots for two months, until he was forced to reduce them.

In the 1830s Macready was manager, but despite his innovations (limelighting, for example, was introduced here), it was financially unsuccessful. In 1847 it reopened as the Royal Italian Opera House but burnt down in 1856.

The present Roman Renaissance building was erected in eight months to the accompaniment of heavy wagers as to its being ready on time. Frederick Gye, the owner and manager, was a man of considerable energy and imagination — he

once proposed to build a covered arcade from the Bank to Trafalgar Square. He persuaded the Bedford Estate to let him build the Floral Hall adjacent as a commercial enterprise to exploit the rising market in flowers — a scheme which failed.

The architect for these dissimilar buildings, the one classical, the other utilising the new-found freedom offered by cast-iron and glass, was the same — E. M. Barry. The Bedford Estate bought back the Floral Hall in 1887 and used it as part of the main market to sell foreign fruit. Until 1940 the Bedfords had their own private box, retiring room and fireplace at the Theatre, reached by a staircase and bridge across one corner of the stage.

The 1920s and 30s were difficult times for Covent Garden Theatre, so much so that the Beecham family, (who had bought the estate from the Bedford family), proposed to Westminster City Council the demolition of the theatre. This was turned down and instead the off-stage facilities were improved with the provision of extra dressing and rehearsal rooms in Mart Street.

During the 2nd World War it was used as a Mecca dance hall, but in 1944 Leslie Boosey and Ralph Hawkes, the music publishers, took a lease

21. The second Covent Garden Theatre, opened 1809, destroyed by fire 1856.

22. Bow Street Magistrates' Court, 1968.

and it was from this arrangement that the Covent Garden Opera Trust evolved, with public money at last being spent on one of the principal opera houses in the world.

There is a plan to expand the complex to the vacant site in James Street, to include another auditorium and a home for the London Opera Centre. *(See Illustrations 20 and 21)*

East Side
Magistrates' Court and Police Station

This Palladian building was erected in 1880 and designed by Sir John Taylor (see No 4 Bow Street for previous history). *(Illustration 22)*

Nos 36/39

In the 1860s No 36 housed a Sick Fund for Actors and Horsemen, a combination one would have thought only obtainable in a pantomime

horse.

The Globe and the Marquis of Anglesey both occupy sites used by pubs since the 17th century. The latter has recently expanded to include No 38 which was a dairy/grocers for about a hundred years.

BROAD COURT

This thoroughfare was largely rebuilt in 1897 by R. S. Wornum, replacing the mid 18th century New Broad Court, which housed a multitude of small trades such as a hatter, umbrella manufacturer, ladies' school and theatrical costumier. Douglas Jerrold, the author of the highly successful play *'Black-eyed Susan'*, lived here as a young man in 1816. At the Wrekin Tavern, formerly on the corner of Broad Court and Crown Court, the

23. *Sir Robert Peel's 'Peelers'. The officer on the right end wears the newly adopted helmet.*

Mulberry Club, very popular with theatre people, was formed and of which Jerrold was a member.

The Fielding Hotel is an 18th century building, or rather a collection of buildings, its name deriving from the nearness of the Bow Street Magistrates' Court and its association with the Fielding brothers.

A plaque at the Bow Street end records the famous residents of the area.

BRYDGES PLACE

The 17th century maps show a series of alleyways between Bedfordbury and St Martin's Lane. Four of them remain, of which Brydges Place is one. It consists now of the side of the Coliseum Theatre and other buildings and has a challenging feel of danger and mystery at night. The name derives from the Chandos family, related to the Bedfords.

BULL INN COURT

This alleyway, between Maiden Lane and the Strand, was built c1635. At the southern end, faced with decorated tiles, is the side door of the Nell Gwynne Tavern, no doubt on the site of the old Bull Inn itself. The Court mainly consists of the sides of buildings. The parish boundary is marked on No 8 where a plaque records that it is part of St Paul Covent Garden; next door another plaque records St Martin's-in-the-Fields.

By the stage door of the Adelphi, William Terris, a well-known actor of his day, was murdered by a stage-hand in 1897.

24. *Burleigh Street, from an illustration in Strand magazine, 1890.*

BURLEIGH STREET

This street was laid out in two phases, the first in 1673 by Lord Burghley across the site of the old Cecil House, from the Strand to as far as what is now Exeter Street. The upper part which connects to Tavistock Street was erected by the seventh Duke of Bedford by 1859 to improve access to the market.

There was once a St Michael's Church at the south-west junction of Burleigh Street and Exeter Street, now part of the Strand Palace Hotel. This was built in 1833 but demolished, with the congregation dwindling, in 1906.

At what was then No 6 in the 1890s, was a printing company called Odhams. This was owned by the father of the Odhams brothers whose company is dealt with under Long Acre.

There are only two buildings of interest left in the street. *(Illustration 24)*

No 14

This is the rectory of St Paul, Covent Garden, built originally in 1860 as a clergy-house for St Michael's opposite. When the church was demolished St Paul's Church took it over.

For its scale and its awkward site it is quite an outstanding building, designed by William Butterfield, making full use of its street angle and impressing with its exterior decoration. It badly needs renovation to bring it back to its small grandeur, but one suspects that its days are numbered despite it being a listed building. A plaque describing its history is set into the wall. *(Illustration 25)*

Nos 11/13

These buildings occupy the corner site with Tavistock Street and were erected in 1860, designed by Charles Gray. They have a very good fascia decoration and are worth preserving, but facing north-east as they do, they get little sun to encourage anyone to devote a great deal of money to them.

25. *No 14 Burleigh Street*

CATHERINE STREET

Catherine Street was built in two parts. The upper part, north of Exeter Street, was laid out in the 1630s and called Brydges Street after the family name of the 4th Earl of Bedford's wife. There was no access to the Strand at its southern end, the way being blocked by the White Hart Inn and the grounds of Exeter House. In 1657 an alleyway to the Strand was formed through the grounds of the inn. When, in 1673, the inn was demolished a street was formed down to the Strand, this part being called Catherine Street, named in honour of the Queen, Catherine of Braganza. It is this later part which was demolished when the Aldwych was built in 1900-5. In 1872 Brydges Street was renamed Catherine Street.

Brydges Street was known as being disreputable for most of its existence, the result, seemingly, of its nearness to the Drury Lane Theatre. In 1787 it was reported that four out of the ten disorderly taverns in the St Paul's parish were here. Fielding in *Tom Jones* and *Jonathan Wild* urges it as a street to be avoided.

There was an emphasis on newspapers and magazines at the southern end in the 18th and early 19th centuries. Titles such as the *Argus, Charter News, Morning Herald* and the *Aera Sunday Newspaper,* were published here. There were wholesale newsagents too. It is reported in *A Bit of Vanishing London* by J. Farlow Wilson, that it was customary for newsvendors to lend the morning papers for an hour each day at a charge of from sixpence to a shilling a week, and to solicit orders from provincial customers to whom papers would be despatched by the evening post, the usual charge being about 24 shillings (£1.20p) a quarter.

West Side
Duchess Theatre

It is difficult to see this building due to the great number of signs advertising the current production. It was built in 1929 to the designs of Ewen Barr, which have undertones of the Elizabethan in the canted bay windows on the upper storeys. It is a pleasant enough building, very restrained, but the architect did not forsee the apparent need to advertise its wares to very myopic people. Its first production had Emlyn Williams in a minor role.

It stands on the site of a house in which John Donne's father lived.

No 19

As the plaque on its frontage says, it was re-erected in 1904, but with no distinction. The reason for its inclusion here is to remark that it has been a restaurant in some form or other for over a hundred years.

No 21

Note the very good mouldings on this building and, as it is a restaurant at the moment, you can view its attractive interior as well. It was a florist's shop since the beginning of this century.

No 23

The Opera Tavern should be admired for its florid frontage. It was built in 1879 and designed by George Treacher, who specialised in pubs; its interior has been spoilt and its bar casement virtually demolished. There has been an inn here probably from the 17th century. Its previous, but not original name, was The Sheridan Knowles. Knowles (1784-1862), was an Irish playwright now forgotten, whose plays were performed at Covent Garden and the Theatre Royal. *(Illustration 26)*

26. The Opera Tavern in Catherine Street.

No 29

The Nell of Old Drury is almost certainly on the site of a 17th century inn which Nell Gywn probably did drink at, but the present building with its bowed front is Victorian. The name is fairly recent, no doubt appended together with a crass inn sign to attract tourists in search of atmosphere, although one would have thought that the old name of Sir John Falstaff would have done, especially as the old inn-sign depicted Sir Ralph Richardson playing the part.

No 33

The bow-fronted shop front is probably typical of this street in the late 18th century. Suttons Seeds have introduced a modern trade-sign outside to give a touch of antiquity, but it isn't very good and they haven't been there long anyway. In the early 19th century it was a coffee-house.

East side

Drury Lane Theatre

Theatre Royal, Drury Lane, is the longest established theatre in the country. In 1662 the Crown granted Thomas Killigrew a patent to manage a theatre, and the following year William Davenant received a similar grant. From these two patents were to develop the Theatre Royal and Covent Garden Theatre which were to enjoy, theoretically anyway, a theatrical monopoly in London for nearly 200 years.

The present Theatre Royal is the fourth on the site. The first building, into which Killigrew's 'King's Company' moved in 1663, was on the site of a riding yard between Catherine Street and Drury Lane. No illustration of this first building (this is the one that Nell Gwyn played at) is known to exist. It was short-lived however, being burnt down in 1672.

It is generally thought that Christoper Wren built the second theatre in 1674, with a major reconstruction by Robert Adam in 1775/6. Its 117 years spanned some of the most famous names in English stage history — Thomas Betterton, Colley Cibber and Mrs Siddons all played here. Charles Macklin appeared in the first revival for years of *The Merchant of Venice* in 1741, to tremendous acclaim; he was also stage manager in the 1730s. David Garrick first appeared here in 1742 as *Lear* and *Richard III*.

27. *Richard Brinsley Sheridan, from a painting by Sir Joshua Reynolds.*

The management, however, had a very mixed career. Christopher Rich, an unpopular and unscrupulous owner who exploited his actors, had the entire company walk out and perform elsewhere in protest at his behaviour. Colley Cibber and Betterton also tried their hands at management but the most famous name in charge was Richard Brinsley Sheridan, in partnership with his father-in-law Thomas Linley, from 1776. *The School for Scandal* was produced the following year.

This second building was demolished in 1791 and a third, much larger, structure erected in 1794, designed by Henry Holland. It was still under Sheridan's management.

The third building had a short life. It was destroyed by fire in 1809 — a damaging blow to the shareholders who had not yet finished paying for it and who had underinsured. The fire was the impetus for a famous remark by Sheridan, who had a financial interest. He calmly watched it burn from a nearby house and said that "surely a gentleman may warm his hands at his own fireside."

Funds to place a new building on the site of this catastrophe were energetically raised by a number of public-spirited individuals, in particular Samuel Whitbread the brewer, but only on condition that Sheridan left.

28. The second Theatre Royal, with its 1775 Catherine Street frontage designed by Robert Adam.

The present building, designed originally by Benjamin Wyatt, opened in 1812, complete with an address written by Lord Byron. Some parts of the building came later — the portico in 1820 and the cast-iron colonnade in Russell Street in 1831. The present auditorium, in Empire style, was made in 1922.

Management and financial loss continued to be problems even with Sheridan gone. In the successful season of 1814, when Edmund Kean made his debut, even then a loss of £20,000 was made and Samuel Whitbread committed suicide. Macready was manager in 1841 but the theatre did not stand on its feet until an impressario called Augustus Harris, with a taste for extravaganzas, took over in 1879.

Henry Irving's famous seasons here were in 1903 and 1905. Ellen Terry celebrated her acting jubilee here in 1905 and Forbes Robertson made his theatrical farewell in 1913. Just before the 1st World War Diaghilev presented two seasons of Russian ballet and opera and, during the war, films were shown, including D.W. Griffiths' *Birth of a Nation*.

The 1930s saw a whole string of successes — Noel Coward's *Cavalcade*, Ivor Novello's *Glamorous Night*, *Careless Rapture*, *Dancing Years*, etc. During the 2nd World War the theatre was used as headquarters for ENSA, the entertainment wing of the armed forces. After the war, musicals made their home here: *Oklahoma!* (1947), *Carousel* (1950), *South Pacific* (1951), *The King and I* (1953), *Camelot* (1964), to name a few. *(Illustrations 27, 28)*

Nos 2/6

These buildings were erected in 1905 and partly occupied by *The Builder* magazine whose editor, H.H. Statham, designed them. The decorated brickwork is a bit unsubtle but they are are an interesting example of the better type of office block being erected in its period. The present occupants of No 6 have installed a metal porch quite out of keeping with the lines of the building. *The Builder* moved away in 1978. *(Illustration 29)*

CHANDOS PLACE

Chandos Place, called Chandos Street until 1937, derives its name from the family of the wife of the 4th Earl of Bedford. Laid out in the 1630s, it is

29. No 4 Catherine Street.

now mainly composed of 19th century buildings. The most significant changes came in 1881 when the Peabody Buildings, the Charing Cross Hospital Medical School and the Chandos Place frontage of the Charing Cross Hospital, were commenced. Originally (as the remaining numbers indicate) there were 68 buildings in the street, including six pubs, of which only the Marquis of Granby and the Welsh Harp remain. The former is listed as being of special architectural or historical interest.

To really stand in a place renowned in English literary folk-lore, go into the rear of the Civil Service Store. There, stand in the food department. This is where the 11-year-old Charles Dickens was consigned to work in Warren's

30. Charles Dickens.

Blacking Warehouse, pasting labels on pots of blacking for six shillings (30p) a week. This was a time of despair for him: his father and mother were in Marshalsea Prison for debt and he was being lodged in Camden Town with 'a reduced old lady'. He walked, of course, to work and he records very sadly "In going to Hungerford Stairs (the location of the warehouse) of a morning, I could not resist the stale pastry put out at half-price on trays at the confectioners in the Tottenham Court Road, and I often spent on that the money I should have kept for my dinner".

Nos 40/42

These premises were occupied from at least 1840, until the early part of this century, by a firm of coppersmiths.

Nos 44/46

For most of the 19th century No 44 was a fire station, strategically placed for a quick dash in a number of directions. Nos 45 and 46 are over an arch leading to Brydges Place, built with immense style and without apology for having no ground floor. Note the decorated late Victorian frontage with its Dutch influence.

31. No. 10 Chandos Place in 1904.

No 61

This was built c1870 on the site of the Ship Inn.

Nos 62/65

Charing Cross Hospital Medical School was built 1881-9, the architect being John Thomson, with some later alterations. Originally Bedford Court (at the rear) gave out into Chandos Place at this point; when the School was built it was incorporated into the building as a passageway, but with later expansion the Court was blocked off.

No 66

This is really the side entrance to Nos 10-13 Bedford Street, the recently vacated premises of J.M. Dent, publishers of the *Everyman* library. (See Bedford Street for building history).

Nos 67/68

This pair of buildings was built in 1868 and are the handsomest in the street with their dominant panelled pilasters. No 68 replaced a pub called the White Swan. In the 1920s they both housed a magazine called *London Opinion*.

CONDUIT COURT

Leonard Cunditt was an inn-holder in Long Acre and this alleyway was probably made by him c1686. It has no architectural interest nowadays but it did contain, till demolition in 1954, two bay-windowed shops on the left (approaching from Long Acre), one of which was a cobblers patronised by Sir Henry Irving.

COVENT GARDEN (THE PIAZZA) AND THE MARKET

The Piazza, or what is known now as Covent Garden, partly surrounded the old market square also called, confusingly, The Piazza. It was designed, almost certainly, by Inigo Jones and built between 1631 and 1637. To the north and east were arcaded houses; the church of St Paul was on the west and some plainer houses and the garden of Bedford House to the south. As a piece of town layout it was unique in this country and the inspiration for all the other London squares still to be built.

It was an instant success and then a general disappointment. The type of tenant the 4th Earl of Bedford had in mind moved on to the new fashionable areas such as Soho, Bloomsbury and St James's. The casual market he had allowed in the square, made legal in 1670, served to drive away this type of tenant. In their place came a social life which revolved around entertainment, the market and wining and dining.

The appearance of the Piazza is shown clearly in illustration 4. Each porticoed residence, different in interior floor plan, had two storeys and dormer above the common, uniform arcade beneath with ground and mezzanine floors fronting the arcade. The photograph of Bedford Chambers (illustration 34) shows a rather larger 19th century resemblance to the original scheme. On the north side were twelve bays on either side of James Street, and on the east, eight bays north and south of Russell Street. On either side of the Church stood a single house without porticos.

This architectural unity disappeared over a number of years. Houses on the south-east side collapsed in 1670, were rebuilt, and then rebuilt again in 1769 without arcades. The house next door to the church on the north side (now part of Nos 1-4 King Street), was pulled down in 1690 and rebuilt, and its twin on the south side of the

church suffered a similar fate in 1729. The westernmost house of the north range, what is now 43 King Street, was demolished and rebuilt in 1717.

In the 19th century the rest of the old buildings came down. Four bays in the north-east corner were demolished in 1858 to be replaced by the Floral Hall. The remainder of that range, from James Street to the Floral Hall, was taken down ten years later to make way for the Tavistock Hotel. In 1879 Bedford Chambers, to the west of James Street, were erected and, finally, the remaining range of original buildings, north of Russell Street, was taken down in 1888.

Shops and stalls began to appear in the arcades in the late 17th century; the first coffee house came in 1726. Together with the immediate vicinity, the Piazza thenceforth took on a character stemming from its nearness to the Drury Lane and Covent Garden theatres, lodging houses and brothels. The southern side, always the poor relation in the enterprise, was fronted with fourteen houses when Bedford House, to their south, was demolished in 1706. During all this time the market was expanding.

In the 19th century the Piazza was given over almost entirely to hotels, some of which still exist in name in other parts of Bedford land — the Tavistock, Bedford and Russell hotels in Holborn being three of them. The siting of hotels here is a retrospective puzzle, for the early morning noise of the market in the 19th century must have been considerable and a significant disturber of the night's sleep.

North-west side

No 43 King Street, originally the westernmost house of the arcade, is dealt with under King Street. Bedford Chambers, on the site of Nos 1-3 Great Piazza (the range south of Russell Street was called Little Piazza) was designed by Henry Clutton in 1879 and built by William Cubitt of Grays Inn Road. At the side of the Chambers, in James Street, are some ornate gates with Covent Garden Warehouses picked out in the ironwork. The present occupiers call it Cubitt's Yard. No 1 became a hotel in 1779 and was eventually to be named Clunn's Hotel, patronized by Douglas Jerrold, a now largely unread author and dramatist. No 2 was a carpet shop from 1757-1876 and

32. The Piazza, east side, with the north-east range in the background. An entrance to Covent Garden Theatre is at the end of the arcade.

in 1777 No 3 became the Gordon Hotel with the Britannia Tavern on the corner with James Street.

North-east side

East of James Street, where the 1930s buildings have just been demolished, was the Tavistock Hotel, built in 1868 and demolished in 1932 when Mart Street was constructed. To the east of this range were Nos 10-12. Sir Peter Lely, 17th century Dutch painter, much favoured by the William and Mary court, lived here and was buried in the churchyard of St Paul, Covent Garden in 1680. He was succeeded as the court's favourite painter by Sir Godfrey Kneller who lived at No 15 Great Piazza.

In 1753 the lessee of this house was Charles Macklin, an actor whose name is remembered in Macklin Street off Drury Lane. He opened the Piazza Coffee House here. It is said that from the top storey of this building Richard Brinsley Sheridan, the playwright, (*The Rivals, School for Scandal* etc) watched Drury Lane Theatre, of which he was part owner, burn to the ground in 1809 with the calm remark that "a gentleman was entitled to warm his hands by his own fireside."

The Piazza Hotel at No 12 was here in the 18th century. It was said to be popular with country gentlemen who desired a meal and a bed with a doxy to share them. The coffee house and hotel disappeared in 1858. Before the hotel, Sir James Thornhill, specialist in painting ceilings, lived here (his work can be seen at the Royal Naval College, Greenwich, Windsor Castle and at Hampton Court). He managed his famous painting academy from 1722-1734 and his son-in-law, William Hogarth, lived here until 1733. (*Illustration 35*)

The eastern range

In the north-east corner Nos 13-14 were the largest house on the Piazza. The most northerly part of the premises became the Shakespeare Tavern with an entrance through to the Opera House at the rear. This very popular rendezvous was said, in its heyday, to employ seven waiters, a cellarman and a boy, that each waiter was well-dressed with ruffles etc, and that they thought they had done badly if they did not each make seven pounds a week in tips. It is stated in the *Survey of London* volume dealing with this area that the tavern was destroyed by fire when the Opera House was burned down in 1808. However, a story printed in *Annals of Covent Garden* by E. Beresford Chancellor, records that the tavern was saved from the fire.

33. Russell Chambers in 1968.

34. Bedford Chambers in 1921. The Tavistock Hotel, since demolished, is in the background.

35. Hogarth's calling card.

Nos 15/17

The more northerly house was the home of Sir Edward Verney in 1634. Fighting for the Royalist cause in the Civil War, he was killed at the battle of Edgehill in 1642. Sir Godfrey Kneller, German-born portrait painter, lived here from 1682-1702. He is known to have painted nearly 6000 works plus 800 unfinished paintings. His portrait of William Wycherley, the dramatist, who lived in Bow Street, is regarded as being one of his best.

The southern part of these premises became the Bedford Hotel in 1802. This was demolished in 1888 and the site has remained open since.

Nos 18/19

Part of these premises, on the corner with Russell Street, became a pub called the Red Lion c1761 and at other times the Russell Hotel. These

36. *Covent Garden before the central market was built. View looking west by F. Nash.*

were demolished in 1888.

South-east range

This site is now occupied by Russell Chambers and part of the old Flower Market. The corner house by Russell Street collapsed in 1670, taking with it the house next door. They were rebuilt in 1681 and shortly afterwards was established, in the range, the first Turkish Baths in this country, called either a 'bagnio' or 'hummums'. In the 18th century the price for bathing was 5/6d (27½p), for two in one room 8/- (40p) and to lodge there overnight cost 10/- (50p). This establishment later became a hotel called the Hummums at which Dr Wolcot (Peter Pindar), Crabbe and Tennyson are known to have stayed. Ladies were admitted but not to the lodgings. It was destroyed by fire in 1769, rebuilt as the New Hummums, but went bankrupt after rebuilding in 1885. Confusingly, another hotel called the Old Hummums opened next door in 1887 on the corner with Russell Street; this was closed in 1892. This latter hotel is now called Russell Chambers and occupied by Tutton's Wine Bar.

Covent Garden Market

The market has now gone to new buildings at Nine Elms, Battersea, leaving behind a social and physical vacuum. Apart from being a genuine piece of London colour it provided employment for many local residents, shelter and scavenged food for many drifters, and a focal point for tourists and visitors. Its principal buildings will be used still, but the cessation of trade brings a breathing space in which they can be restored.

The market was at its busiest in the early hours of each morning when fruit, vegetables and flowers came into the traders and then went out again, profit made, to shopkeepers and dealers. Congestion in the square and streets around was a way of life at both day and night. The buildings were not large enough to cope with the modern volume of trade or the methods of handling produce; adjacent roads were inadequate to take lorries.

It was inevitable, and in fact long planned, that the market should move, much to the distress of those who would wander down in the early hours to sniff the atmosphere. Sightseers are unlikely to make their way to Nine Elms.

It was twice as large as any other market in London, Smithfield excepted. It was unique in that it was privately owned until 1962 and still subject to tolls by its owner — a fact that attracted political attention for at least a hundred years. This private ownership, for 248 years vested in the Bedford family, and then for 44 years in the Beecham family, meant that significant financial resources, especially those of the Bedfords, could be found, without recourse to democratic discussion, to finance its continuous regeneration. It is suggested that one of the reasons for the market's longevity is that the Bedford's ownership of the surrounding area enabled the market to expand as it needed.

A passage from a book by Charles Dickens jnr conjures up the late 19th century view of the market:

'All night long on the great main roads the rumble of the heavy waggons seldom ceases and before daylight the market is crowded. The very loading of these waggons is in itself a wonder, and the wall-like regularity with which cabbages, cauliflowers, turnips are built up to a height of some 12ft is nothing short of marvellous. Between 5 and 6 o'clock the light traps of the greengrocers of the metropolis rattle up, and all the streets around the market become thronged with their carts, while the costermongers come in in immense numbers. If it be summer-time flowers as well as fruits are sold at the early markets. Then there are hundreds of women and girls among the crowd, purchasing bunches of roses, violets and other flowers, and then sitting down on the steps of the church, or of the houses round the market, dividing the large bunches into smaller ones, or making those pretty button-hole bouquets in which our London flower-girls can now fairly hold their own in point of taste with those of France or Italy . . . On each side of the main avenue (within the central market building) are enclosed squares and here the wholesale fruit market is carried on. In winter there are thousands of boxes of oranges, hundreds of sacks of nuts, boxes of Hamburg grapes and of French winter pears, barrels of bright American apples. At ten o'clock the sale begins; auctioneers stand

37. Covent Garden soon after the central market was erected 1828-30

on boxes, and while the more expensive fruits are purchased by the West-end fruiterers, the cheaper are briskly bid for by the costermongers.'

A 20th century outsider would have found it just as busy, noisy and attractive. But in reality its time had come — it could no longer cope with the demands presented to it.

The first recorded mention of the square being used for market purposes is in 1654. Illustration 4 shows it in c1720 when wooden rails had been erected round the square and traders kept themselves to the southern side.

In 1670, 40 years after the residential area around it had been laid-out, the fifth Earl of Bedford was granted authority to hold a market here, the right extending to him and his heirs for ever. The right to levy tolls was not sufficiently stated but always claimed and, unusually, a specific area approximating to the square was authorised. When later Dukes attempted to levy tolls on market goods sold outside this area much resentment was caused and eventually, as new leases came up, this right was written into agreements as a legal protection for the Dukes.

The Earls and the Dukes of Bedford leased out the market franchise, sometimes on only a yearly basis. This generally meant that management of its affairs went to the highest bidder, not necessarily the most competent.

Gradually shanty shops filled the square and trade expanded until it became the focal point for the large number of market gardens around central London. It drew in a good deal of casual labour such as ill-paid Irish women who were able

38. A market scene in 1965.

to walk for miles carrying on their heads up to 1cwt of produce. It attracted too, with its nearness to the two theatres, many brothels and a disreputable name. *(Illustration 36)*

The Central Market Building

To replace the assortment of buildings on the square a proper market was built in 1828-30 to the designs of Charles Fowler, a specialist in market buildings. This is the central building which, with modifications, still stands. It was mainly built by William Cubitt of Grays Inn Road who also added the glass roof in the 1870s and 1880s. To erect this building an Act of Parliament was obtained and the opportunity was then taken to regularise the Duke's right to collect tolls. This central hall has now been converted to house an assortment of shops. *(Illustrations 8 and 37)*

Congestion and access were serious problems. There were bars across Southampton and Burleigh Streets, and Maiden Lane, to prevent market traffic. King Street and Bedford Street at their western ends led out into what is now called New Row, a very narrow highway. To the south, by the Strand, Bedford Street was narrow and still is. The only adequate access to the north was through James Street and Long Acre. Faced with this the Duke of Bedford aided a scheme to build Garrick Street in the 1860s and at last there was a proper road through to the west-end of London.

The Flower Market

The flower trade was not properly housed. This led the Duke to build a temporary structure on the south east (outside the old limited area) and a permanent building, again built by Cubitt, was put up in 1872, to be extended even further to Bow Street in 1885.

This has been converted to provide a home for the London Transport Museum and the National Theatre Museum.

The Floral Hall

In 1856 Covent Garden Theatre burned down and its manager obtained a lease from the Duke of Bedford to build a larger theatre and also, in its rear, a flower market: the Floral Hall stands there still. It is odd that a theatre manager should want to branch out in such a way, and even odder that the Duke agreed to what could have been a rival

concern. In the event it was a financial failure and in 1887 the Duke bought the building and turned it into a foreign fruit market, though the old Floral Hall name was confusingly kept. *(Illustration 39)*

The Jubilee Market

The last addition was the Jubilee Market on the south side, now housing stalls selling clothes etc. and a sports hall. This was erected in 1904 to sell foreign flowers. The present plan, strongly opposed, is to demolish this market.

Sale of the Market

This 19th century building programme had proceeded at a time when the Duke's ownership of the market and his right to collect tolls were under sharp political criticism. Tired of it all by 1907, the then Duke of Bedford was negotiating to sell Covent Garden. He had been unsuccessful earlier in trying to sell out to the Metropolitan Board of Works (forerunner to the LCC and GLC) and, failing them, to the City of London. In 1913 he found a buyer at a price of £2 million who then, a year later, sold for £250,000 his option to buy to Sir Joseph Beecham, St Helens manufacturer of the famous Beecham pills. Terms were agreed for the sale to Beecham, but then the 1st World War broke out and the movement of this sort of capital was prohibited. After the war the deal was concluded although Sir Joseph had died in the meantime.

Control of the market and the whole Bedford estate in Covent Garden, excepting two houses, was then vested in the Covent Garden Estates Company principally owned by Sir Joseph's two sons, Sir Thomas, the famous conductor, and his brother Henry. The two sons then proceeded to what we would now call 'asset-strip' their purchase. Properties were sold off so that eventually just about only the market buildings were left. These they sold to the publicly owned Covent Garden Market Authority in 1962 for £3,925,000.

Thus the market, at last and to most people's relief, came into public ownership in time for its next phase of development.

39. The Floral Hall, south range.

CROWN COURT

The northern part of this passageway was called
Cross Court in the 19th century and up till then
did not join what is now the southern part. The
only significant building here is the Scottish
National Church, built in 1909, and designed by
Balfour and Turner in an undistinguished neo-
Elizabethan style. There is an entrance to the
church through a passageway built within the
entire length of the Fortune Theatre in Russell
Street.

DRURY LANE

Nowadays Drury Lane is the least interesting,
architecturally, of the main Covent Garden
thoroughfares. There are few stylish buildings
and to picture Drury Lane at its height, or at it
seediest, is to require imagination.

It is thought to be, at the least, a 12th century
lane, originally called Via de Aldwych. In the 16th

century Sir Roger Drury erected a mansion here,
called Drury Place, in what was known as Wych
Street, an eastern arm of Drury Lane which led
down to Temple Bar. This turning was obliterated when the Aldwych was built in 1900. In the
16th century, and later, Drury Lane terminated
near the Strand to continue through a narrow
alley called Little Drury Lane.

The Aldwych Theatre straddles the site of
White Hart Yard which led through to the stables
of Bedford House and before that was probably
the eastern gate into the old convent garden.

From the 17th century Drury Lane was the axis
for numerous alleyways and courtyards on both
sides. Nell Gwyn lived in Drury Court, an alleyway south of Drury Lane leading to the Strand.
Pepys records in his 1667 diary a walk to Westminster: "In the way meeting many milkmaids
with their garlands upon their pails, dancing with
a fiddler before them; and saw pretty Nell Gwynn
standing at her lodgings' door in Drury Court in

her smock sleeves and bodice looking upon me; she seemed a mighty pretty creature."

Pepys also records the outbreak of the Great Plague in Drury Lane in 1665. In June he records: "This day much against my will I did in Drury Lane see two or three houses marked with a red cross upon the doors, and "Lord have mercy upon us" writ there; which was a sad sight to see, being the first of the kind that, to my remembrance, I ever saw."

It goes without saying that the narrow courtyards off Drury Lane had a very bad reputation indeed. In the late 19th century social change came. More supervision of the granting of leases on the west side was exercised. At the southern end, the Theatre Royal extended its premises to have a rear entrance (note the large doors to take scenery). St Clement Danes National Schools were built opposite Siddons Buildings and the Aldwych scheme, begun in 1900, obliterated a great deal. So in the space of about 20 years the old nature and reputation disappeared. The Inns of Court Mission (Nos 44/6) were built in 1904 with castellated turret and cupola and are now the Gainsford Sports Club.

The reputation and the fame derived from the Drury Lane Theatre (see Catherine Street). By the time the New London Theatre was built (1972, architect Paul Tvrikovic), a requirement when the old Winter Garden Theatre was demolished in the early 1970s, that sort of cultural life was firmly centred in the West End and on the Strand. Any new theatrical venture that far up the Lane was probably doomed to failure and so it has proved. Also on the New London site has been the Middlesex Music Hall, an early 19th century enterprise, and at No 173 the first shop owned by John Sainsbury, founder of the well-known grocery firm. *(Illustration 40)*

Sainsbury opened this shop in 1869 when he was 25. The house had three floors, an attic and a basement, and he and his wife Mary, who he had married the same year, lived above the shop. She herself was the daughter of a dairyman whose shop in Chalton Street, Somers Town, eventually became a Sainsbury branch. Sainsbury's childhood was spent living near the New Cut street market, Waterloo, just by the Old Vic theatre. His first job was helping in a grocery shop there. So, he was well used to market trading and the

40. No 173, Drury Lane, Sainsbury's first shop. From an old and crumpled postcard.

competition permanent shops faced in such situations. His second shop, in Queen's Crescent, Kentish Town, was within another street market and it was here that he built bacon stoves and stabling.

The unusual feature of the Sainsbury expansion was that the shops were widely scattered — Croydon, Balham, Brondesbury and Kentish Town were early branches. This must have entailed a great deal of tedious travelling for someone managing a one-man business, even though supported by a working wife. But still, she had six sons and six daughters and life must have been hard.

The Croydon branch set the house style, well laid out with marble counters, tiles on floors and walls, good woodwork throughout and above all — a distinctive feature — well lit by gas. Sainsbury's last words before he died in 1928 were "Keep the shops well lit", a measure of his dedic-

41.Drury Lane in the 1870s. Picture by the Society for Photographing Relics of Old London.

42. Ancient houses, Drury Court.

ation to the business. The shops were what we would now call 'up-market', serving a wide variety of clientele. Great emphasis was placed on cleanliness and freshness, an obsession with Sainsbury which his sons and grandsons have nurtured to this day.

Sir John Barbirolli, the conductor, lived, according to him, at No 37, now a listed building, from 1901 to 1906. Aptly enough he was above a music-smith's shop.   In 1840 there were 18 pubs in Drury Lane, sandwiched between the many small trades and shops. Today there are only three — The Sun, White Hart and the Marlborough Head. The White Hart was there at least by 1570 and the present building strives hard to convince us of its Tudor upbringing. In a room above, Karl Marx spoke to a meeting of the German Workers Educational Society in November 1847.

At No 35 is the firm of A. Butler & Sons, ironmongers, who have been here since the 1930s. Their original blue and white sign is still there advertising gas, steam and hot water fittings.

The oldest business in the Lane is, unusually, a shoe shop — Jackmans at Nos 188/9. John Jackman, shoemaker, set up shop here c1860. However, the most unusual shop is that of Philip Poole at No 182, which specialises in pen-nibs. *(Illustrations 41 and 42)*

DRYDEN STREET

In the 17th century Dryden Street was Middlesex Court. It was largely rebuilt in the 19th century and widened, becoming Wilson Street. In 1938 it was renamed after John Dryden, poet, (1631-1700), born of a Puritan family and who became a Catholic on the accession of James II, a conversion many thought sincere rather than convenient. He lived in Long Acre and used to walk most nights to Will's Coffee House at No 1 Bow Street, where he was the central attraction in a seat specially reserved for him by the fire in winter and by the window in summer.

The street comprises of undistinguished industrial premises. No 5 houses a number of craft workshops.

EARLHAM STREET

Earlham Street crosses Seven Dials and therefore only a half, known previously as Great Earl Street, comes within the scope of this book. Seven Dials was an ambitious building plan devised by Thomas Neale (see Neal Street), Master of the Mint, in the last seven years of the 17th century. Seven streets, of which Little and Great Earl Streets were two, radiated from a doric column surmounted by sundials. In 1773 rumour swept town that treasure was buried beneath the column. It was promptly dismantled — no treasure was found — and re-erected at Weybridge Green.

The area was described by Charles Dickens in memorable terms, particularly in *Sketches by Boz* (1834). His son, Charles jnr, more prosaically had this to say: "Children sit on doorsteps and on the pavement, they play in the gutter, they chase each other in the road, and dodge in and out of houses. It is evident that the School Board has not much power in the neighbourhood of the Dials. Public houses abound, and it is evident that whatever there may be a lack of in the Dials, there is no lack of money to pay for drink. At night the public-houses are ablaze with light, and on Saturday evenings there is a great sound of shouting and

43. The junction of Earlham Street and Shelton Street, c1820.

singing through the windows, while the women stand outside and wait, hoping against hope that their husbands will come out before the week's money is all spent. Nowhere within reach of the West-end of London can such a glimpse of the life of the poorer classes be obtained as on a Saturday evening at the Dials.''

This area was adjacent to the equally notorious Rookeries of St Giles.

Nineteenth century trade consisted mainly of secondhand goods and remained unsubstantial till the end of the century, so that the street directories didn't bother to record them. Lepard and Smiths, paper merchants, now removed like the market to the Nine Elms area, were its first major firm in the 1920s. Their old building at No 42 still has their lion insignia on the fascia.

One of the old warehouses, No 43, has been converted handsomely to provide the British Crafts Centre with a home. *(Illustration 43)*

ENDELL STREET

Oddly concentrated in this street have been buildings devoted to keeping us morally and physically healthy. The explanation must be that it was built in 1845, roughly on the line of Belton and Hanover Streets, just at about the time the zeal to help the poor and wayward was burgeoning. Its building linked up with that of Wellington Street into the Strand, so that there was henceforth a throughway from Waterloo Bridge to Shaftesbury Avenue.

Large parts (the least interesting) of Endell Street have been demolished and building work is going on at both ends so that it is difficult to feel

44. Endell Street Workhouse, later called Dudley House.

much affection for the street at the moment. But it has an interesting array of buildings, most of them neglected.

Aptly enough the street was named after a Rector of St Giles who cared very much for the welfare of the poor, James Endell Taylor. The street was planned by Sir James Pennethorne, who was responsible for several London street innovations such as Victoria Street and New Oxford Street — he seemed to delight in pushing new roads through old slums.

At what used to be 23/25 (now part of a re-development site) at the corner with Shelton Street on the west side, was a building containing 'Queen Anne's Bath' a place said to be frequented by the Queen. It was almost certainly a turkish bath establishment, fed by a spring cut off in the 1840s.

West Side
No 31
The Cross Keys has one of the best looking pub fronts in Covent Garden, including cherubs cross-

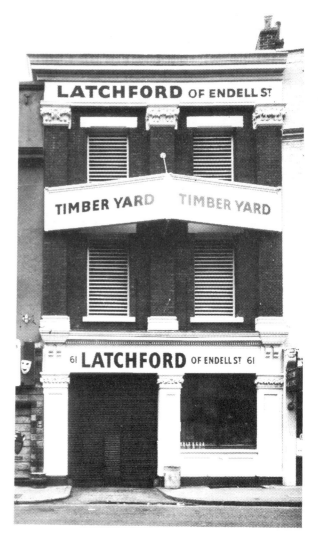

45. Latchford's Timber Store, Endell Street, in 1974.

ing keys in stone. The interior is worth seeing too — every scrap of wall is covered with print or painting. It is as old as the street and its present immaculate state surrounded by the dirt of re-development is a credit to the owners. In the 1860s the Burton Brewery had premises next door to the south.

No 39
Diana's Diner is well-known in Covent Garden — very good cheap food. The original occupant made rocking horses, but for the last sixty years it has been dining rooms.

No 61
This interesting building was erected for

Latchford's Timber Merchants who still occupy the premises. Built in red brick and faced with stucco at ground floor, it has very dominant features. The windows have heavy wooden louvres to aid the seasoning of timber. An excellent building to look at. *(Illustration 45)*

No 71

This is a very distinctive industrial building with great assurance about it — note the very heavy dormer window. Presumably people used to look above ground level more in those days — how else would you explain features like this, intended for admiration, or advertising high on buildings intended for notice?

Swiss Protestant Church

This 'incorrect Palladian' building, as Pevsner decribes it, was built in 1853, and designed by George Vulliamy. It was paid for by Swiss residents in London and replaced their old place of worship in Moor Street, Soho. Inside, it is very austere. *(Illustration 46)*

London Central YMCA

The YMCA occupy the former St Giles National Schools built in 1859 and designed by E. M. Barry — the words National School are still on the brickwork. On the day it opened 900 children attended, yet the playground was only 40ft square. If you like Gothic buildings it is quite a good one, but it needs a good clean.

East Side

The Oasis

The modern swimming baths (1960) replace the old Bloomsbury and St Giles Baths and Wash-houses built in 1852. In their rear, the St Giles Workhouse later renamed Dudley House was still there at the turn of this century. It was recently demolished. Just south of the housing scheme site, was Christ Church, demolished in the 1930s. *(Illustrations 44 and 48)*

St Paul's Hospital

This teaching hospital, specialising in urology, occupies the old British Lying-In Hospital, the oldest Lying-In hospital in London. It was founded in Betterton Street in 1749, moving to this building in 1849. It has very striking window

46. The Swiss Church, Endell Street.

frames, especially on its flank wall.

No 22

The main feature of this now empty building is the way that the pointed arches of the windows are then compromised by a lower, flatter lintel. It was built for a stained-glass manufacturer — the trade can just be picked out on the fascia if you know it already. Succeeding businesses made razor strops and cases. In the basement remain two glass furnaces, one late 18th century, the other late 19th century. The architect was a Mr Withers. *(Illustration 47)*

47. *Stained Glass Manufactory, Endell Street.*

48. *Endell Street baths, early 19th century.*

EXCHANGE COURT

A magnificent, little known, house exists here, just being renovated. It is Nos 1-5 and was the headquarters of the Corps of Commissionaires, an organisation founded, as the plaque at the Strand entrance proclaims, in 1859 by Captain Sir Edward Walter. The Corps is principally devoted to providing men of good character to act as guardians of property — they present a much more welcoming face than the newer security firms possess. It began as a way of providing employment for wounded soldiers but now generally employs pensioned servicemen.

The Court takes its name from Exeter Change, a trading establishment, in the Strand. *(Illustrations 49 and 50)*

49. *Exchange Court. An 18th century watercolour.*

50. Nos 1-5 Exchange Court.

EXETER STREET

There is very little of interest in Exeter Street. It is dominated by, as it were, the inner functions of the Strand Palace Hotel, with a footway above road level, and the back of Tower House (see Southampton Street).

It was built in two parts, the first in 1673 laid out by Lord Burghley, which stretched from Catherine Street on the east to just beyond the footbridge on the west. By 1708 the Bedfords had extended it west by building an alley called Denmark Court. In 1831 it took its southward turn to the Strand. It takes its name from Exeter House (previously Cecil House), which stood on the site of the Lyceum.

Its most notable resident was Dr Johnson, who lodged here in 1737 when he first came to London, with Richard Norris, a staymaker. The site of this house is now covered by Wellington Street where it meets Exeter Street.

On the north side, facing Burleigh Street, there were once premises called the Boars Head, then rebuilt as the Royal Panopticon Institute of Science in 1851. For at least twenty years it was the printing works of the *News of the World*, another indication of this area's specialisation in the publishing business.

In 1842 there were complaints about a brothel in this street run by a Mrs Crutchley 'where scenes of the grossest infamy are daily exposed. The house appears to be the resort of women of the lowest description whose screams throughout the greater part of the night keep the neighbourhood in a constant state of annoyance. Cries of murder have made it necessary frequently to call in the Police. Women in a state of almost perfect nudity and drunkenness are constantly exposing themselves in the yard of the said premises...' A far scream indeed from today's lifelessness in this street.

The only building of note is the Old Bell Tavern and that is really part of Wellington Street.

FLORAL STREET

Floral Street was inaptly named as it was, until 1974, dominated by the fruit trade. Previously it was called Hart Street until 1895. Architecturally, it is without much interest other than nos 12 and 24. It is fairly derelict and is the one street in Covent Garden which could be largely rebuilt with small-scale buildings. Even No 29, which used to be a pub, betrays no evidence of its past.

It was laid out by 1637 as part of the Bedford Estate plan. The south side served principally for stables and coachhouses for King Street, but gradually the whole street became one of small traders and warehouses. By 1840 it still had a cowkeeper there, though fields were at some distance.

Originally it was a cul-de-sac at its western end, where past No 24 was blocked by the back garden of No 29 King Street and access to Long Acre or King Street was provided through various alleyways still there today. When Garrick Street was built in the 1860s the present extension of Floral Street was made, but its character as a back road has not changed; its narrowness has prevented it from being a particularly desirable address. In 1829 there were complaints about dunghills here, and in the 1840s about brothels, especially at the Bow Street end.

No 12

This is a building which strives to impress with style in a street where it is difficult to stand back and admire it. It was built as a school in 1838 and altered substantially in 1860, which is the date emblazoned on its frontage. There was a school

51. No 24 Floral Street in 1968.

for poor children on the site in 1751. This newer building, called the Adelphi School, was arranged so that no noise should penetrate to King Street, by the simple expedient of having no windows at its rear and side; also the children were not allowed to play in the back courtyard and, presumably, played nowhere outside at all. The Vestry's good intentions were hampered somewhat by No 11 being in 1842, a brothel, and in 1847, a cowhouse. By the 1860s it was called Covent Garden Market School and in 1899 it was closed. From 1900 to 1918 it was used as a club (religiously guided) for market workers. In the 1920s the fruit trade had taken it over and this was the position until just before the market moved out. Then the Dance Centre, still there now, used it as their premises. To the rear there is a solarium for ladies only.

It is a fanciful, Italianate building with an outside staircase in the turret structure at the front, now accommodating a lift.

No 24

This is a good, plain example of industrial architecture, built in 1859 by William Howard, the local builder, and designed by C. G. Searle. Its most prominent occupant has been Strand Electric whose offices were at the rear in 29/30 King Street. (*Illustration 51*)

52. Nos 46/47 Floral Street

Nos 46/47

These small houses were built in the 1830s — note the mansard roofs. They have retained their character despite being taken over by the fruit trade in the 19th century. (*Illustration 52*)

No 52

This was built in 1838 and was originally the residence of the local surveyor of pavements. Its frontage has been spoiled by the café.

GARRICK STREET

Garrick Street, named after the actor David Garrick, was formed in the 1860s to improve access to Covent Garden market. Apart from No 7, which had a shoe-polish manufacturer here for some time, it has always had what would be called a good class of tenant.

No 14

This building, now the Inigo Jones restaurant, always occasions comment, not the least because

53. No 14 Garrick Street in 1967.

it has been restored so well. A first guess that it might have had some ecclesiastical use before would be right in two senses. It was originally (1860) a mission house and school, but soon after became the factory of Heaton, Butler and Bayne, stained-glass manufacturers. When they moved out after the last War, it came into multi-use, including the King Street Club.

It was designed by Arthur Blomfield and he has used that most effective combination of yellow and red bricks fashionable at the time (No 21 Wellington Street uses the same contrast). It has a mixture of very definite pointed arches and straight lintelled windows that unexpectedly works. The bold way it sweeps into Floral Street underlines just how badly architects handle corner sites nowadays. *(Illustration 53)*

Nos 18/24

This group has a richly decorated front with classical stone figures, typical of the period. Nos 18-20 have the original shop front but the National Westminster Bank has ruined the rest.

West Side
The Garrick Club

This austere, and certainly very dirty, building was opened in 1864, designed by F. Marrable. The Club had previously been round the corner at No 35 King Street. It possesses a well-known collection of paintings and portraits, many related to the theatre, but you have to be a member or guest to see them. The collection includes paintings by Zoffany, Lely, Kneller and Moreland senior.

The much publicised quarrel between Dickens and Thackeray occurred here in 1858, after Dickens had supported another club member, Edmund Yates, who had written a rather scurrilous article about Thackeray. The estrangement between these former friends lasted for five years until they met by chance on the hall steps of the Athenaeum Club and spontaneously shook hands. *(Illustration 54)*

Nos 9/13 and 17/21

These striking buildings have unusual proportions in that above the ground floor, the first floor is squat, the second elongated and the third repeats the squatness of the first. There are some decorated classical figures in the semi-circular

54. The Garrick Club in 1967.

heads to the second-floor windows but their height above street level prevents one from appreciating them easily.

No 11 has its original, delicately decorated shop front. It is occupied, (and has been all this century), by C. & W. May, theatrical costumiers, now a subsidiary of Moss Brothers.

No 1

The Round House pub on the corner was, until the last War, Petter's Hotel and before that the Bassett Hotel. Note the three-dimensional inn-sign outside, crude but welcome.

GOODWINS COURT

This is one of the gems of Covent Garden and, indeed, of London. It is so easily missed, that a determined effort must be made to see this alley-way running from Bedfordbury to St Martin's Lane, and since the restaurant Giovanni's positioned its front door here more people have been astounded to find the Court.

It consists of two rows of cottages, some with bow windows. A modern plaque on a wall, draw-

55. Goodwin's Court in the 1950s.

ing upon the authority of the *Survey of London*, states that they were built c1690, but Pevsner dates them late 18th century. They were condemned as residences in 1936 but allowed for office use. They are all in better condition now, probably, than they have ever been, with good street lamps. If the owners of Nos 13 and 14 could be persuaded to remove the rendering on their premises, the old brickwork would be virtually complete throughout. You can enter the passageway through an arch between Nos 23 and 24 Bedfordbury — the other entrance in St Martin's Lane has been modernised. Look back to the rear of the Bedfordbury houses — a good Olde London view with a modern clock.

That this Court should have survived almost intact is quite remarkable, for it would have had no social cachet and was probably very unhygienic for most of its existence. In the 19th century it was occupied by a colony of tailors. *(Illustration 55)*

GREAT QUEEN STREET

Great Queen Street is dominated by freemasonry. The massive Hall, the Connaught Rooms, the buildings for the Royal Masonic Institutes for Girls and Boys, all emphasise the central presence of freemasonry in grandiloquent style. The street lost its more intimate nature when these absurdly impressive buildings came. It needed only the insensitive Elizabethan House horror at the eastern end to put the street completely off-balance.

There was a recognised pathway here certainly in the 16th century and it was a route by which James I reached one of his residences, near Theobalds Road. The street was built in the first half of the 17th century — of brick, and was therefore regarded as the 'first regular street in London'. It was named after James I's queen, Anne of Denmark.

The organised history of freemasonry in this country stems from the foundation of the Grand Lodge in 1717. They opened their first building here in 1776, having taken over two houses on the site of the Connaught Rooms. Extension proceeded westward for a hundred and fifty years, culminating in the present Freemasons' Hall.

Early 19th century directories show Great Queen Street to be a usual mixture of small trades

56. Nos 27/28 Great Queen Street in 1977.

and pubs, with some emphasis on the coach building trade as an extension to Long Acre. This mixture, excepting the coachbuilding, still applies.

North Side
Nos 4 and 6

Both are late 18th century and have been used for a variety of trades, especially coachbuilding at No 4, where the fascia of the Blitz drinking establishment completely disregards the scale of the building. *(Illustration 59)*

Nos 8-18 Elizabethan House

This overbearing building (1961, John Burnett, Tait and Partners, architects) replaced two pubs, a theatre and some 19th century buildings. The pubs, The George and Hercules Pillars, have been replaced in the new complex on the sites they have had since, probably, the street was built.

In the 1860s the site of No 8 was a Refuge for

57. *The Novelty Theatre, later the Kingsway Theatre, Great Queen Street, in 1904.*

58. Nos 10/11 Great Queen Street in 1904.

59. No 4 Great Queen Street in 1904.

Homeless Boys and this, in 1882, became the Novelty Theatre which opened with a comic opera. This theatre had the distinction of changing its name eight times in its first 14 years, four of these changes being a return to the original. In 1900, with a reconstructed interior, it became the Great Queen Street Theatre and then in 1907 the Kingsway. It was damaged in the war in 1941, remained derelict and was demolished in 1956. *(Illustration 57)*

No 13, during the 1860s and 70s, was the office for the sale of Parliamentary Papers — the forerunner of the present day Stationery Office in Holborn. *(See also illustration 58)*

Nos 19 to 21

Messrs Toye, Kenning and Spencer, suppliers of masonic goods, are an amalgamation of three old established businesses, all begun by masons.

William Henry Toye, a braid and lacemaker, is listed in the 1880s in Old Ford Road, east London, as a masonic supplier, and he had moved to Theobalds Road by the 1st World War. George Kenning, masonic publishers, had premises at Little Britain and 198 Fleet Street, then at 16

Great Queen Street in the 1880s till the 2nd World War. In the meantime, they branched out into ribbons, military and otherwise, in a very Dickensian shop near the Old Bailey. Richard Spencer sold masonic books at No 26, then 23a and later at this address from the 1920s.

No 22

The premises of Louis Cornelissen, artists' colourmen, contain one of the most harmonious shop interiors in London — marvellous cabinet fittings and bottles abound. The business was founded by Cornelissen in this building in the 1860s.

Nos 24-26

The Royal Masonic Institute for Boys was built at the turn of this century.

Nos 27 and 28

These two houses are early 18th century survivors with handsome Doric doorways and mansard roofs. No 27 has been a masonic lodge since 1917. *The Survey of London* records an ornamental lead cistern at No 27 dated 1733. *(Illustration 56)*

Nos 30/31

The Royal Masonic Institute for Girls was built c1925 on the site of two houses used by coach-builders.

No 32

L'Opera Restaurant have installed a Ye Olde Worlde shop front. There has been a restaurant here since the 1930s; before that it was a pawn-brokers for a hundred years.

Nos 33-38

Nos 33 and 35 are early 18th century. The good shop front of No 33 is counterbalanced by the appalling one on No 35. Very sad. Nos 36-38 are late 18th century.

No 40 The Sugar Loaf

Probably on the site of a 17th century pub but it is difficult to estimate an age for this present structure. It appears to have increased its size (it took in No 39 in 1972)

South Side

Connaught Rooms and Freemasons' Hall

The original Freemasons' Hall and Free-masons' Tavern were built on the site of the Connaught Rooms in 1776. The Freemasons then extended both eastwards and westwards, taking over Bacon's Hotel at Nos 64/65 and building the Mark Masons Hall, and westwards again in 1866, to erect a new Hall. A further western wing was added in 1899.

The Connaught Rooms replaced the Tavern and the old Temple after the 1st World War. The present Freemasons' Hall complex, for all the world like some giant liner berthed here, was completed in 1933 by Ashley and Newman. *(Illustrations 60 and 61)*

HANOVER PLACE

This passageway runs between Long Acre and Floral Street and consists of the sides of other buildings. It was built in 1637 and then called Phoenix Alley. A tavern here was called the Crown (later the Ship). It was kept by John Taylor (1580-1653), known as the Water Poet for his literary support for the dwindling cause of the Thames watermen — their right to ferry people from one end of London to the other was threatened by coaches. He achieved fame by a voyage from London to Queenborough, Kent, in a paper boat. His poetry is pretty awful.

60. The old Freemasons' Hall in 1904.

61. The new Freemasons' Hall in 1956.

HEATHCOCK COURT

The best way to see this Court is to come in from the Strand entrance. Despite the rather overwhelming white-tiled entrance it takes little imagination, going up towards Exchange Court, to picture a 17th century network of courtyards. Burgoyne House faces you at the top end, clearly built on the line of a 17th century house and an old Wine Lodge is on the left.

HENRIETTA STREET

This street, named after Charles I's queen, is mainly 19th century and has been, since then until recent times, a home for publishers. It was laid out in 1631 and was bascially a good-class shopping street with residents above. It is said that Lord Strafford, scourge of the Irish in the 17th century, subsequently executed on the order of Charles I, lived on the south side, but the location is unknown.

Despite its situation it never did, apart from two buildings, become involved in the market trade. It once had five pubs but these were gradually suppressed by the Bedfords and none exists today. The Castle Tavern which stood on the north corner with Bedford Street (the site of Alginate House), was the scene of Sheridan's duel with a Mr Matthews who had insulted him, or his lady, in the *Bath Chronicle*. It is also recounted that here one gallant, after filling the shoe of one of the ladies present with wine, drank it and presented the sodden shoe to the cook who made a ragoût from it, later consumed. Nos 24 and 25 were both coffee houses in the early 18th century and it was at No 25 that a meeting took place in 1754 which led to the formation of the Royal Society of Arts.

South Side
Nos 1/2

This bank building was erected in 1878 as the Covent Garden Hotel.

Nos 3/4

These were built in 1784. No 4, the plant shop, has kept its handsome door but lost its frontage, no doubt in the years that a market trader occupied it. No 3 has been the home of two of our most famous publishers — Duckworths from the turn of the century until the 1950s, when they were followed by MacGibbon and Kee, two firms now merged with larger concerns.

Nos 5/8

These premises have 19th century fronts on 1731 buildings — the earlier houses had collapsed. Since the 1830s Nos 5 and 6 have been occupied by a series of banks culminating in the present Barclays. Curtis Brown, the literary agents, were upstairs from 1903 to the 1950s.

Nos 7 and 8 are being renovated but still have a dignified Ballière Tindall sign on their fascia. This firm dealt in medical books from the turn of the century and the last Tindall, the father of novelist Gillian Tindall, recounts that a ghost haunted the place. Previous occupants of these buildings included the St Paul's rector, a solicitor and physician, so it is, no doubt, a well-spoken ghost.

Nos 9/10

No 9 was erected in 1727, its first tenant a mercer, and No 10 in 1726, leased to a linen draper. The shop fronts, matching but now altered, were installed from 1861. In 1807-16 No 10 was occupied by the bankers Austen, Maunde and Tilson of whom Jane Austen's brother was a partner. She stayed here while visiting London in 1813 and 1814. Until recently it was used as an Institute of Urology by St Peter's Hospital opposite. *(Illustration 62)*

No 11

This has very strong Dickens connections, being the premises of Chapman Hall, his publishers, from the 19th century until the 2nd World War.

Nos 12/13

Above the door are the initials AH intertwined, witness to its previous use as Ashley's Hotel when it was built in 1879 on the site of a smaller version. By 1903 it had become Goschens Buildings and used by a variety of small publishers and advertising agencies. It is in Italianate style and retains some good railings. Originally it had a rear entrance in Maiden Lane.

No 14

Victor Gollancz, the publishers, are still here today. Gollancz established his business in 1927 and was famous for his *Left Book Club* in the 1930s and for his cheap, yellow-covered general

62. No 10 Henrietta Street in 1938.

range of books. Before him were Williams and Norgate, equally well-known in their period. The house, erected 1875, has an elaborate oak shopfront with an imposing doorway.

Nos 15/16

This Anglo-Dutch building, designed by H. E. Pollard, was erected in 1888, for the Strand Union Office, an organisation which dealt with the poor relief in the area. By 1923 it had become a registry office.

Nos 17/18

These were built in 1892 and were the premises of C. Arthur Pearson, one of the most famous popular magazine proprietors in the late 19th century and slightly beyond. He began his journalistic career at Newnes, eventually his main rival, where he became manager. On leaving, he founded *Pearson's Weekly*, *Home Notes*, *Short Stories* and others, magazines which exploited the

new but uncultivated literacy. In 1900 he founded the *Daily Express* and in 1905 he owned the *Standard* and *St James's Gazette*. Soon after 1910, he became totally blind and thereafter devoted his energies to the welfare of the blind. He founded St Dunstan's for blinded soldiers and sailors.

A wrought-iron frame still hangs from the front of the building — the missing sign no doubt being Pearson's. Another distinctive feature is the tiled frontage.

North Side
No 22

This handsome building was once called Woburn Chambers — a name which flows more freely from the tongue than Alginate House, the present title. Still, it is a striking building, taking full advantage of its corner site. The architect was Charles Gray, one-time *enfant terrible* of the architectural profession, who helped to found the

63. Alginate House, Henrietta Street, in 1968.

Architectural Association at the age of 18. It was built in 1858 and mainly used by solicitors, which probably explains the 'Chambers' in the original name. *(Illustration 63)*

Nos 23/24

This pair of buildings was built in 1886 — their first tenants were the Theatrical Mission. Offleys, a famed chop-house was at No 23 from 1840 followed by Macmillans in 1863. The buildings continued to be used by various small publishers until the 1970s. They have a dreadful new frontage.

St Peter's Hospital

This hospital, specialising in urology, was founded in Marylebone in 1860. It moved here, to these new premises, in 1882. It seems a peculiar place to locate a hospital, as the early morning noise from the Market must have been anticipated. Even today it has a warning notice forbidding the stacking of market trucks outside. It is designed by J. M. Brydon in Norman Shaw style. *(Illustration 64)*

No 31

The lessee of this early house agreed to make a passageway through his ground floor to the churchyard behind to replace the one that had been a feature of the earliest house. This access is

64. Nos 25-29 Henrietta Street, St Peter's Hospital

duplicated in the corresponding house in King Street.

No 34

Originally, as with No 1 King Street, a house stood facing the square, flanking the Church. This present corner block, designed by Alfred Williams, was erected in 1890 for the London and County Banking Company.

HOP GARDENS

Hop Gardens is named from a hop garden in the vicinity owned by Sir Hugh Platt in the early 17th century. He himself lived in Bethnal Green but also owned land in Kentish Town. The passageway is one of a series running from Bedfordbury to St. Martin's Lane and has been largely rebuilt. In the 1840s it housed four shops which specialised in woollen drapery.

65. Inigo Jones.

INIGO PLACE AND ST PAUL'S CHURCH

Inigo Place is named after Inigo Jones, the architect of St Paul's Church and the overall designer of the original Covent Garden scheme. Jones was born in 1573 and travelled widely in Italy. He was much influenced by the architecture he saw — he introduced pure Renaissance into this country. He was, at the time of Covent Garden's construction, Surveyor-of-the-King's Works to Charles I, who took a great interest in the Covent Garden scheme. Whether the King insisted that Jones should be the architect for the Church, or the Earl of Bedford thought it prudent to appoint him anyway, is not known. In fact, it is not known as an absolute certainty that he was the architect, but there is hardly a doubt. The uncertainty is caused by the lack of a recorded payment to him in the Bedford archives.

Inigo Place, off Bedford Street, leads from a fine pair of 1789 gates to the churchyard and the entrance to St Paul's church. A door on the right leads to a flat, previously the home of Ellen Terry's daughter. The churchyard, now gardens, is an ideal place to have a sit down, especially on the seats donated by the now departed market traders. Around you are the backs of the buildings of King and Henrietta Streets. Originally the brass statue of Charles I, now in Trafalgar Square facing Whitehall, was positioned here.

The Church, described later, is known as the Actors' Church, due to the large number of theatrical people either buried or remembered here. But other well-known people have been interred either in the churchyard or church, though actual memorials are in short supply.

Robert Carr, Earl of Somerset and favourite of James I, was buried here. Carr finished his life under a cloud. Both he and his friend Sir Thomas Overbury fell in love with the Countess of Essex, who thereupon attempted to obtain an annulment of her marriage to Essex so that she could marry Carr. Overbury opposed this plan. As a result he

66. St. Paul's Church, east side, in 1968.

was imprisoned in the Tower on a trumped-up charge and died there, it is thought, from poisoning. The annulment was procured, Carr and the Countess were married, but gossip about Overbury's suspected murder reached scandalous proportions so that justice had to be seen to be done; this was especially so once Carr had been superseded as favourite by Villiers, Duke of Buckingham. So, justice was done in a half-hearted way. Alleged accomplices were executed, the Countess was imprisoned for two years and Carr from 1616-22 before obtaining a Royal pardon. The Countess and Carr subsequently lived in married disharmony.

Other people buried here include Sir Peter Lely, painter (d1680), William Wycherley, dramatist and resident of Bow Street (d1715), Charles Macklin, actor (d1797), Grinling Gibbons, artist (d1721), Tom Davies, actor and bookseller who introduced James Boswell to Dr Johnson (see Russell Street), Samuel Butler,

satirist, who lived in Rose Street (d1670), John Wolcot, satirist (usually known by his pen-name Peter Pindar (d1819), Thomas Rowlandson, artist (d1827), and Thomas Arne, composer, born in King Street (d1778). There is some doubt as to Charles Macklin's birth date but he died either aged 97 or 107. He once killed a fellow actor in a green-room quarrel, with a stage dagger. He was lucky to be acquitted and continued acting into his nineties. In a macabre way the memorial to Macklin in the Church records this incident, in that the inscription was crowned with a theatrical mask which had a dagger through the eye.

Claud Duval, the famous highwayman, was laid and delivered here simply because he was caught in nearby Chandos Place. He terrorised Holloway and Islington in particular and until the 19th century there was a Duval's Lane in Holloway.

Other actors remembered here are Charles Cochrane, Ivor Novello, Leslie Henson, Vivien Leigh, Ellen Terry and Bransby Williiams.

67. Interior of St. Paul's Church, 1968.

68. *Grinling Gibbons, from a painting by Sir Godfrey Kneller.*

69. *Sir Peter Lely, from a painting by himself.*

70. *Dr John Wolcot.*

On the outside of the Church, by the vestry door, there is a memorial to Henry Mosse, Rector of the Church, who was killed in an air raid in Long Acre in 1918 while ministering to his parishioners.

J.M.W. Turner, the artist, born in Maiden Lane in 1775, was baptised here (his parents had been married here too). W.S. Gilbert, the librettist, was baptised here in 1837.

The Church, one of the first built for Protestant worship, was begun in 1631 as a chapel-of-ease to St Martin's-in-the-Fields and was consecrated as a parish church in 1638. Horace Walpole in 1765 published the well-known anecdote about its early days. 'When the Earl of Bedford sent for Jones, he told him he wanted a chapel for the parishioners of Covent-garden, but added he "wou'd not go to any considerable expense; in short," said he, "I wou'd not have it much better than a barn." "Well then" replied Jones, "you shall have the handsomest barn in England." Jones fulfilled his promise.

It is a rectangular building, 100ft x 50ft, and its plain interior is without division. Its most marked exterior features are the widely overhanging eaves and the Tuscan columns supporting a very deep portico. The *Survey of London* has revealed that it was originally intended to have the main entrance at the east end of the Church, necessitating the altar being at the west — quite contrary to prevailing Church views. During the building operations the plan was changed so that entry was

from the west but Jones kept to his architectural logic and harmony and retained the glorious semblance of entry from the Square. In recent times an inner door has been installed at the western end which many would think is totally out of keeping with the rest of the building.

The church was gutted by fire in 1795 soon after considerable renovation had been completed and one year after the insurance policy had lapsed. The disaster was caused by plumbers leaving a fire unattended during a meal break. The walls stood but the interior was rebuilt very near to the original design, and by 1798 the work was complete. The architect for this rebuilding work was Thomas Hardwick, who had seen his earlier renovation perish in the fire.

There used to be seven steps down from the portico to the market square, an indication of how much the level of the square has been raised over the years though these steps were not to be found during the recent works which stripped the surface of the paving. It is said that the father-in-law of Lord Archer, a Mr West MP, (both of whom lived at 43 King Street), had difficulty in dismounting from his carriage because of the old pavement level. On hearing of this the Covent Garden surveyor agreed to raise the level of the pavement outside, thereby obliterating the steps, but this does not seem a very likely story.

On the Piazza side of the Church is an inscription which tells us that the first performance of the puppet show featuring Punch

71. *St. Paul's Church, west side, 1979.*

took place in the square in 1662. Also, of course, the portico is the setting for the opening scene of Shaw's *Pygmalion. (Illustrations 65, 66, 67, 68, 69, 70 and 71)*

JAMES STREET

This street has been affected most from its involvement with the market, its use as an access road, and periods of demolition. It was built in the 1630s and like most of the main streets in Covent Garden, lost its titled residents very soon. By the 1840s, there were market traders here and far more in the 1860s, so that by the beginning of this century, it was almost entirely concerned with the fruit trade. *(Illustration 72)*

No 10

There has been a pub called the Nags Head here since the 1670s. The present building was erected in 1900 in neo-Jacobean style, its present decoration probably smarter than it has ever been.

No 21

This is now a betting shop but used to be a pub called The Grapes.

72. *Nos 8-9 James Street in 1968 (now demolished).*

Nos 28/29

These are the only early 18th century buildings left in the street and still proclaim their recent use by market traders. Charles Grignion, the engraver who did work for Hogarth, lived at No 28 1750-72.

KEAN STREET

Edmund and Charles Kean (father and son) were both actors associated with the Theatre Royal, Drury Lane, in the first half of the 19th century. Edmund's first appearance was with Kemble and Sarah Siddons at the age of 12 in *King John*, but his fame was based on his Shakespearian roles, particularly those of Richard III, Hamlet and Shylock. Drink made his last years impoverished. His son Charles followed in his Shakespearian tradition.

Kean Street, a 19th century road, was named in the 1920s. Its main feature is on the east side, where spectacular commercial buildings have massive sloping roofs containing three storeys with prominent windows. They are most unusual.

73. Keeley Street (then Little Wyld Street) in 1903.

KEELEY STREET

Keeley Street, laid out in 1690 and known as Little Wild Street until 1905, has little of interest. The late 19th century school on the Wild Street corner, now part of the City Literary Institute, is on the site of Weld House (see Wild Street).

Robert Keeley (1792-1869) born near here, was a comedian at the Theatre Royal, Drury Lane. (*Illustration 73*)

KEMBLE STREET

Kemble Street is another of the streets in the area named after Drury Lane actors (Keeley, Kean, Betterton and Macklin Streets are others). Until 1877 it was called Princes Street, a name which went in the general tidying up of duplicated street names at that period. It is a 17th century thoroughfare which crossed what is now Kingsway to Duke's Street.

The Kemble family was prominent on the stage of Drury Lane in the late 18th and early 19th centuries. The father, Roger, was a strolling player, his daughter became Sarah Siddons, and his son John played Shakespeare at Drury Lane. Another son, Charles, became manager of Covent Garden Theatre in 1822 and Charles' daughter Fanny (later Mrs Butler), acted and wrote plays. It is interesting to note that Maria Kemble (an Austrian actress unconnected with this Kemble family) appeared at Drury Lane in 1786, and in 1792 played Macheath, of all roles, in *The Beggar's Opera*. (*Illustration 74*)

Kemble Street is now entirely composed of Peabody Estate buildings (c1880) and Bruce House, a lodging house for the homeless.

KING STREET

Almost every building in King Street is worth looking at. The Earl of Bedford, naming it in honour of the monarch who had granted him the licence to build (Charles I), intended it to be the principal street, an adornment to the Piazza. It was laid out in 1633. King Street, like the rest of Covent Garden, fell victim to developments in Bloomsbury, Soho and St James's, and quickly lost its titled residents, settling down to become a good-class residential and trading street. By the 20th century it was very down-at-heel, its fascias obliterated by shutters. A great deal of it is late 19th century and third generation building, but it

74. *John Kemble ('the last likeness ever taken') by Sir T. Lawrence.*

is built with such style that it will blossom in this present transitional stage.

It is still a bit of a mess, needing a mixture of personal enterprise and strict control over the ground floor fascias. No 40, for example, the Banco de Bilbao building, has an awful new shopfront quite out of keeping with its architecture. There are still a number of derelict properties needing affectionate and sensitive restoration and it is the street's good fortune to be renovated at a time when people worry about such things.

South Side
Nos 1/4

Originally No 1 was part of the Piazza, a house facing on to the market square, but without the ground floor arcade common to most of the Piazza. This house was the first to disappear in 1689 and the new house was rebuilt again in 1754 for an organ builder. The present Nos 1-4 were erected in 1884, designed by Henry Clutton, the Duke of Bedford's consultant architect who built Bedford Chambers opposite a few years earlier.

In the 19th century, these houses were let out to small traders like basket makers, booksellers and clothiers, but after the rebuilding in 1884 they became the premises of George Monro, one of the prominent market traders, and a clothier. By 1935 the old LMS Railway had taken over Nos 3 and 4 for a booking office, a facility kept on by British Rail, who eventually took the whole block — a site, one feels, not particularly suited to them. It is now the headquarters of the GLC's Covent Garden Development Team, which one can visit to obtain information. There is, however, a very disappointing lack of literature there to explain what is going on.

Nos 5/6

These premises were built in 1874. No 5 was occupied by a succession of accountants and insurance brokers for most of this century and is now derelict. No 6, Penny's Wine Bar, is an old pub called the Essex Serpent. This 17th century inn derived its name from a report from Saffron Walden, Essex, which described a 'sighting of a Monstrous Serpent which hath divers times been seen at a Parish called Henham-on-the-Mount within four miles of Saffron Walden'. Penny's Wine Bar is a recent name.

No 7

This was rebuilt in 1896 and the architect merely extended the frontage of Nos 5 and 6. It, together with No 8, was a costumiers for most of this century.

No 8

Part of the ground floor has a gateway, fronted by a gate into St Paul's churchyard, a feature duplicated in Henrietta Street. Some kind of passageway was probably here from the start.

No 9-11

Take no notice of the numbering painted on the shop fronts — the present occupiers appear to have missed out No 10. *The Saturday Review,* a popular 19th century publication, was housed at Nos 9 and 10. No 10 has a theatrical history, being in 1903 the headquarters of the Actors' Association and in 1923 an early home of the British Drama League. Later on it became one of the many Italian cafés in the area. No 11 was taken over at the turn of this century by a seed merchant and its deterioration probably began then.

Nos 12/13

The present occupiers confusingly call this Nos 10-13. This pair of buildings was erected in 1874 and Barrs, the seedsmen who occupied No 11 as well, were the tenants. In 1965, Curtis Brown, the well-known literary agents, were here after their move from Henrietta Street.

No 14

An Italianate building with probably some of the early 18th century structure left, but mainly 19th century now. From 1860 to the 1930s, it housed a picture dealer and then became a café. It is now derelict.

No 15

This was built in 1775 and occupied by button makers until 1885. It was then used by publishers, first the *Whitehall Review,* until the 1970s.

75. Nos 29/30 King Street in 1972.

76. No 26 King Street in 1968.

No 16

This corner building is the headquarters of the Communist Party of Great Britian and has been since the 1920s. The lower facade is awful. Ironically its neighbours round the corner in Bedford Street have included Debretts and that master of property development Richard Seifert, architect.

North Side
No 26

On the corner is a very handsome building going mainly into Garrick Street which indicates the old line of King Street before Garrick Street was built. Originally, traffic from King Street exited through the narrow New Row opposite, a cause of much congestion.

This much-praised building, now empty, was built for the auctioneers Debenham, Storr and Sons who had occupied part of this site since 1813. When built it had a magnificent mahogany rostrum in the auction room but this has, no doubt, disappeared in the renovation. *(Illustration 76)*

No 27/28

These two buildings, with a common frontage, have been occupied by insurance companies since

77. Nos 27/28 King Street in 1967.

the mid 19th century. No 27 was originally built in 1760 and sold to the Westminster Fire Office, who had been before in Bedford Street, in 1808. They remodelled the front in 1853 to be more attractive to the public and three years later they acquired No 28 and duplicated the frontage there. On the front of No 27, and being kept in the renovation, is an impressive cartouche of the Prince of Wales' Feathers. Underneath was the wording WESTMINSTER FIRE OFFICE on a sill band, recently obliterated, an inscription repeated on its side wall round the corner in Rose Street. The building has very fine ironwork at ground and first floor levels. After a succession of mergers and acquisitions it has become the offices of the Sun Alliance Insurance Co. In 1840 No 28 was occupied by manufacturers of gambroons, which appear to be a kind of shooting jacket. (*Illustration 77*)

Nos 29/30

These two buildings have had interesting occupants since the mid-19th century when they were built with matching shopfronts — unfortunately No 30 has all but lost this adornment. By the 1860s No 29 was occupied by a firm of stationers, called Lepard and Smiths, who even today are suppliers of paper to the printing trade. In 1913 it was the home of the *Guardian* newspaper (not the present one), and in the 1940s Strand Electric, well-known suppliers of lighting to the theatrical business had its headquarters here. No 30 was built for Hamburger Rogers, a firm of gold-lace manufacturers. They were followed by James Willing, an advertising agency, publishers of Willing's Press Guide, a directory of this country's newspapers and magazines, still published. By the 1930s it was given over to the fruit and veg trade until Strand Electric extended their premises here in the 1960s. Rank Strand Electric carry on that connection today. (*Illustration 75*)

Nos 31/32

No 31 was built in 1713 and refaced, with No 32, in 1860. The first occupant was Thomas Arne, upholsterer, father of the composer, Thomas jnr. The latter was born in the previous house on the site which was destroyed by fire in 1710. He had been intended for the Bar but his love of music overrode this and he produced his first opera when he was 23. He is, of course, the composer of '*Rule Britannia*' which was part of a masque called '*Alfred*'. In 1744 he was appointed composer to the Drury Lane Theatre. He was buried in St Paul's churchyard.

From the mid 19th century, Nos 31 and 32 were occupied by Verity's, a well-known company at the time, who were progressively described through the years as brass-founders, gas-fitters and electrical engineers — undoubtedly a firm which moved with invention. Both buildings became part of the fruit and veg trade by 1939. They still retain good iron balconies.

No 33

This is still derelict and badly needs renovation. It has been the home of bootmakers, booksellers, a magazine called the *British Architect* and a cinema organ manufacturer, before succumbing to market use.

No 34

This has a splendid door and unusually thin and stylish window pillars. It was, from the 1880s to the late 1950s, the home of publishers, in particular Rivingtons.

No 35

This is now empty but recently sold. It was built in 1866 for Stephen Smith, a silversmith. The ornamentation on the front of the building has been removed. The Garrick Club used it as its first home before it moved to its sumptuous Garrick Street building in the 1860s.

No 36

This was built in 1715 and substantially altered in 1751, when it was occupied by a tailor. It was used by a market trader in the 1930s.

No 37

Built in the late Palladian style in 1774. The first occupant was a lawyer called John Lane, who was active in establishing the parish workhouse. William Howard, a builder responsible for many of the 19th century premises in Covent Garden, lived here from 1863-79. Captain Wombwell then brought his Fielding Club here.

No 38

This dates from c1774 and its principal use has been as an auction room, mainly that of J. C. Stevens, from 1776 to the 2nd World War. Even rare orchids were auctioned here. A large showroom was built at the rear in the late 18th century.

The first auction business here was begun by Samuel Patterson, who produced the first auction catalogues. John Crace Stevens became the owner in 1834, but it was his son Henry who made the rooms famous, assuming control at the age of 20 when his father died.

The Africa Centre now occupies the building with a shop, cultural centre and restaurant.

No 39

The front of this building has been drastically altered and is now the Grange Restaurant. In common with most of the houses in this street it became a shuttered fruit and veg place in the 1930s.

78. Rustic Smoking Promenade at 42 King Street in the 18th century.

No 40

The front of this mid 18th century building has been stripped of all its features and adorned with the sort of shop front that gives banks a bad name. In 1754 it was occupied by Moses Mendes, a poet long forgotten, and in 1757 by Lord Chedworth. The Banco de Bilbao came here in the early 1960s.

Nos 41/42

Like Nos 1/4 and Bedford Chambers, these buildings, now a Chinese restaurant, were designed by Henry Clutton and built in 1877 by William Cubitt. It was originally tenanted by a linen-draper, but by the turn of the century George Monro, one of the largest market dealers, had taken it over - hence Monro House on the brass plate. *(Illustration 78)*

No 43

Thomas Archer House is the prize building in the street — and in Covent Garden, excepting only the Church and the Market Hall. On this site was originally the westernmost house of the arcaded Piazza, but it was one of the first to be taken down in 1716. The old house had been inhabited by Admiral Edward Russell, grandson of the fourth Earl of Bedford, who played a leading part in bringing William of Orange to the throne of England. He was created Earl of Orford in 1697 and later made First Lord of the Admiralty. A plaque commemorating his residence is on the front.

The present house, built in 1717, has had a history that, in theory, should have defeated its architecture, but it still resembles closely outside, since renovation, the early prints. (Its development can be seen in Illustrations 79, 81, 82 and 83). It had a stable and coachhouse fronting on to Floral Street at the rear.

The architect was Thomas Archer, who later married into the Orford family and inherited the building, to become an unusual case of an architect daring to live in his own house. A contemporary opinion of the house describes it as 'one of the most expensive and worst in London', an example of criticism to stifle one's own faculties. It ceased to be a private house in 1772, when it was opened as the Grand Hotel for wealthy clientèle able to pay 15 shillings (75p) a night for two rooms. An opening (side entrance) was made into the arcaded walk but the present side door into Bedford Chambers, c1877, is now obsolete.

By the 1840s the house was owned by W. C.

Evans, an actor, and was known either as the Grand or Evans' Hotel. The basement was turned into a late-night rendezvous for singing and supper. The next owner, Paddy Green, built in four months, an elaborate music hall at the rear on the garden (see illustration 80) and this lasted until the National Sporting Club, tenants from 1891-1922, used it for boxing tournaments. The hall is now replaced by warehousing and the Solarium in Floral Street.

After the Sporting Club, Messrs George Monro (see Nos 41/42) occupied it, and pushed a drive-way through its centre so that a warehouse they had built at the rear could be reached from the road. Thus the magnificent oak stairway in the hall, now re-erected in a house in Norfolk, was removed, together with the porch and the pillars. In their place a shutter was put. In 1934 the upper

79. No. 43 King Street, early 18th century.

80. *Evans' Music Hall at the rear of 43 King Street, in 1855.*
From the Illustrated London News, 26th January, 1856.

81. *Evans' Grand Hotel, No 43 King Street.*

82. No 43 King Street c1932.

83. No 43 King Street in 1968 when its front entrance connected to a warehouse at the rear.

floor was sublet to the Players' Theatre and later the New Players' Theatre. Peter Ustinov appeared here in his younger days.

The building was rescued when George Monro moved out to the new market. A new front and inner door and the present, not very convincing pillars were installed. Inside, the walls were painted Wedgewood green throughout and the Board Room on the first floor, with its magnificent plaster mouldings, fireplace and chandelier, brought to its former glory.

The Board Room is the extent of its real interest inside, however, and the view from the back over the tatty warehouse is depressing. It is occupied by a well-known advertising agency, KMP Partnership.

LANGLEY COURT

In the 17th century this passageway off Long Acre was called Blackamoor Alley. It was later called Leg Alley, probably after the Golden Leg pub then on the corner with Long Acre. It is now named after Sir Roger Langley of the Inner Temple, who had land in this area in the 18th

century. It is now devoid of architectural interest but illustration 84 is worth looking at.

LANGLEY STREET

Langley Street was probably built c1700 on the grounds of a house owned by Sir Roger Langley of the Inner Temple, whose property stretched from Long Acre to Shelton Street. In the 19th century it was almost entirely devoted to the carriage-making trade as an adjunct to Long Acre, and now consists of 19th century industrial premises.

LONG ACRE

Long Acre never was an acre — it was a narrow seven acre strip of land north of the Convent garden and south of the Mercers' Company estate. The word 'acre' was being used either in its old sense, meaning field, or else it meant a strip in a much larger field at the time of open-field farming.

The Long Acre came into the hands of the Convent of St Peter, Westminster, together with the main Covent Garden estate, in the Middle Ages. Subsequently, in 1536, it passed to Henry

84. *Langley Court in 1911.*

VIII and in 1552 to John Russell, Earl of Bedford. It was laid out for building in 1615, and it was required that the houses should be built 'substantiallie and stronglie and in a convenient decent and comelie forme, and three stories in heigth (yf not above) and the forepart or front thereof at the least of brick'. This applied to the south side, part of which, between Banbury Court and Rose Street, was sold to the Earl of Pembroke in 1618, later, in 1650, passing to the Earl of Salisbury.

Thus Long Acre, owned by several absentee landlords and most of it let piecemeal on building leases, had a quite different building history to that of Covent Garden proper.

In the 18th century Long Acre was established as the centre for the coach and carriage making trade. Pepys had already recorded that he had gone to Long Acre to buy a coach so, presumably, this speciality had settled here when the fashionable moved to Covent Garden and remained even when they moved to adjacent areas like Bloomsbury and Soho. The 1840 Street Directory records 35 firms in Long Acre involved in the trade. Its influence was felt in surrounding streets as well, with small shops making the lace and upholstery and ornamental painters earning a living. The motor car changed all this in the early part of this century although Long Acre was the home of some car-dealers, notably British Mercedes at 127-130. The premises vacated by the carriage trade were eagerly taken up by the fast-growing market traders, and by Odhams Press, whose buildings came to dominate the street. One

85. No 137 Long Acre in 1903.

firm which has to be noted in connection with carriages, is that of Merryweathers at No 63, who made fire engines here from the early 19th century to the 1950s.

Two large areas between Arne Street and Neal Street are now demolished, both in their latter days being part of the printing and publishing headquarters of Odhams Press.

The growth of Odhams is a classic rags-to-riches story. In 1894 two Odhams brothers set up a small printing business in Floral Street — their father already had a similar business in Burleigh Street. The machinery was antiquated, facilities poor and business hard to attract. After considerable persistence by a young man called Julius Salter Elias, they took him on that year as office and errand boy. The firm continued to do badly and closure was imminent, when the brothers, as an experiment that would have happened only in those days, appointed their office-boy as manager.

Elias set about getting business with the dedication to work and lack of care for himself that was to mark his whole life. He was obsessed with the work, not only getting the orders, but checking meticulously on quality and accuracy. He was aware that the way for the firm to survive was to obtain regular contract work in the form of magazines. Gradually all sorts of specialist publications were printed at their small Floral Street works — *Physical Culture, Racing Pigeon, The Family Doctor* and *Vanity Fair* were some. Some magazines folded very quickly and left bad debts, but it was a gamble that Elias was prepared to take.

By 1906 Odhams badly needed more space. Already a great deal of their work was produced by arrangement at another firm of printers and new premises had to be obtained. They moved into the Queen's Theatre which stood at 93 Long Acre, with splendid Ionic columns outside. Originally St Martin's Hall had been on the site in 1850, but in 1867 two newspaper proprietors built the theatre which seated nearly 2000 people. It lasted for 11 years and it was here that Henry Irving and Ellen Terry first met — a theatrical relationship that was to have an important place in English theatre.

When the place closed as a theatre it housed a variety of trades. Odhams shared it with Spicers, the paper manufacturers, who stored reels here, a

86. *The Bird in Hand, Long Acre, viewed from Conduit Court.*

seed merchant who had part of the Royal Circle, contractors to the Post Office who had the pit and so on — a conglomeration and working arrangement unthinkable nowadays. Gradually Odhams began to fill the building.

The turning point in the firm's history was the contract to print the magazine *John Bull*. The journal became a legend in publishing history. It was founded by a flamboyant MP called Horatio Bottomley whose life style was a scandal and subject of envy. He dabbled in many things, but he had imagination and that magnetism which persuades people to part with their money and excuse his faults. His popular following was immense, his business deals shady. *John Bull*, owned and edited by him, was an instant success. Its style was racy, its contents attracted writs by the score. It set out to expose corruption and mis-government with a directness that, perhaps, would make even the editor of *Private Eye* blanch. The trouble was, as far as Odhams were concerned, that he didn't pay his bills and eventually the company had to take over the management of the magazine to ensure that they got their money. Circulation reached 1,700,000 copies, a size unequalled in this country till then. Subsequently, the unpredictable Bottomley was bought out and Odhams became editorial controllers. Sales plummeted to 300,000, but Elias persevered and gradually the figure went up to a million again, a reverse of fortunes entirely due to the courage of Elias.

In the meantime he took on other publications. He began the magazine *Ideal Home*. He bought rotary machines to print the *People* newspaper, then on hard times. *Picturegoer* was developed by him and then he bought *Sporting Life* and branched out even more, to own the largest bill-posting company in this country.

At about the same time the TUC had taken over the *Daily Herald,* a struggling publication which had begun as a strike sheet by printers in 1911. In an unusual deal, Odhams bought 51% of the shares, leaving the TUC 49% and control of editorial policy. The *Herald* was a massive success, at one time the largest selling daily and engaged in a spectacular war of gifts and insurance policy incentives with the *Daily Express* and *Daily Mail*. The *Daily Herald* is now called the *Sun* and its politics are a long way from what they were.

Elias's next major plunge was to buy photogravure machinery from America for a new factory at Watford. To feed the machinery he invented magazines such as *Woman* (1937) and *Illustrated* (1939),the main rival to *Picture Post*.

Elias became Viscount Southwood. He lived simply and without ostentation in Highgate, working very long hours every day. Odhams Press survives him but its domination of Long Acre has gone.

The most famous resident of Long Acre was John Dryden who lived on the north side facing Rose Street. It is said, too, that Oliver Cromwell lived on the south side from 1637-1643; this is possible, as he was an MP at the time, but unproved.

Nos 12/14
Edward Stanford set up his map business here c1880 but this present building with its rich exterior reliefs and large gable was built c1901 by Herbert Read and Macdonald.

Nos 15/17
This is probably the dreariest, most insensitive and inappropriate building in Covent Garden — well done both client and architect! There was, until 1954, an attractive pub called the Bird in Hand on the corner with Conduit Court, before it was demolished to make way for this appalling structure. No criticism of this new building should be muted and petitions to demolish should be sent to the GLC. *(Illustration 86)*.

Nos 22/23
Harvey's Auction Rooms occupy one of the most attractive premises in the street, only two storeys high. They were previously the home of coachmakers, motor body builders and then fruit and veg merchants.

Nos 24/25
In 1863 the occupiers of No 24 were lighthouse engineers and there they continued until car dealers took their place early this century. It has a plaque with the initials CH on it — derivation unknown.

Nos 30/31
Some buildings in Long Acre are listed for their special interest. Oddly enough this one isn't and it is one of the most distinguished in the road. It was built c1870 of red and yellow brick for a firm of coachmakers called Richard Strong. Note the very fine spiralled window supports.

Nos 32/33
The fascia tell us that it was built in 1862. The occupants then were Charles Windover, carriage-makers.

No 34
The modern Kings Arms supersedes an older version which in the 1850s succeeded the Long Acre Coffee Rooms.

Underground Station
The tube station, opened in 1907, is faced with traditional red tiles and is very much of its period, except for the more modern upper storeys. Its

interior is undistinguished, except for some art deco ironwork above the lift doors.

Nos 46/49

These buildings, vacated by market traders, are fairly derelict. At the end of the last century Nos 48/49 were occupied by the Newport Market Refuge and Independent School.

Nos 51/54

Of these two Victorian buildings only No 53 is listed. No 52 was the headquarters of Hazell, Watson and Viney, now a very well-known firm of printers at Aylesbury. This firm's fortunes were made, initially, in 1851 when they obtained the contract to print the *Band of Hope Review* at the height of the temperance boom.

Nos 57/59

This stylish Edwardian block housed yet another part of the Odhams empire. Their premises covered the site of a coachmakers workshop.

No 63

Until the 1950s this was the address of Merryweather & Son, who made fire engines here for at least a hundred years previously.

No 66

The Sun tavern, with its richly decorated front, is best viewed from across the road — a fine example of mid Victorian pub building. No pub existed here before.

87. No 138 Long Acre in 1903.

South side
Nos 78/79
These 18th century buildings are listed as being of special interest. Brodie and Middleton, artists' suppliers, have been here for over a hundred years and still retain their old shop-front.

Nos 81/82
Originally the Freemasons Arms (probably a late 18th century pub) occupied only No 81 with a coachmakers at No 82. The inscription on the fascia gives the date of rebuilding as 1896; the opportunity was then taken to dress it up with Freemasonry symbols.

No 116
Paxmans, the musical instrument suppliers, have been here only a few years. Their shop window is a delight, as too is their trade sign hanging outside. In the 19th century the premises housed carriage frame makers and a market trader took it over in the 1920s.

Nos 120/123
This Edwardian building is on Mercers' Company land — their saintly lady insignia is there. The Banco Espanol have followed the tradition of the several Spanish banks in the area and clothed their shop-front in unlovely marble.

Nos 127/130 and 132/137
The high arches of these buildings, apart from being fashionable at the time, probably once featured large doors so that the original occupants, carriage makers, could wheel out their merchandise. *(Illustrations 85 and 86).*

LUMLEY COURT
A completely undistinguished Court, originally 17th century, but not opened into Maiden Lane until 1870.

MACKLIN STREET
Macklin Street began life as Lewknors or Lutenors Lane in the 1620s, one of the most disreputable streets in London. Sir Roger L'Estrange, writing in 1715, mentions it as being a 'rendezvous and nursery for lewd women first resorted to by the Roundheads'. All this area down to Seven Dials, was one of poverty, taverns and brothels. Captain Macheath in *'The Beggars Opera'* is procured, by an innkeeper, a lady from

88. *Charles Macklin, by Opie.*

here. Retribution came — the late 19th century saw it begin to change into a street of good works so that it is now dominated by 'artisans dwellings'.

The present buildings are too high for the width of the street but this probably wasn't much of a consideration in the circumstances. At Nos 1-7 the W. H. Smith Memorial Building (1892), now very run down, provides accommodation for organisations carrying on that 19th century social work and those early reformers would be sad indeed to see down and outs sleeping in its porchway, wrapped in whatever they can wear or carry. The W. H. Smith Trust had, as its principal function, the provision of youth clubs.

At 17a are the St Giles Almshouses, removed from Smarts Place, and at No 25 is what appears to be a 19th century mission hall. The St Joseph Roman Catholic Primary Schools are a reminder of what school buildings used to be like.

Called Charles Street by then, the street was

renamed in 1878 after Charles Macklin, 18th century actor, who performed at the Theatre Royal, Drury Lane. *(Illustration 88)*

MAIDEN LANE

The narrowness of Maiden Lane is a reminder that it was once a trackway skirting the edge of the Convent garden, leading down to Westminster. The derivation of its very old name is uncertain. It was laid out in 1631 and originally had no opening at its eastern end, where it came up against the wall of Bedford House, which stood on the site of Southampton Street. Although a pedestrian way was made through to Southampton Street in 1706, it was not made accessible to traffic until 1857, but even then had a bar across it until 1872 in an attempt to prohibit market traders using it.

Most of the street is rather plain 19th century, but despite its lack of grandeur both now and earlier, it has housed at least four of Covent Garden's most famous residents.

The English landscape artist J. M. W. Turner was born at No 21, on the south side, in 1775. The site is now derelict. His father, William Turner, was a hairdresser who subsequently lived together with his son, at No 26 *(Illustrations 89 and 93)*. Part of No 21 was used for exhibitions by the Free Society of Artists — premises later used by the Maiden Lane Synagogue. In the basement of this house was a pub called the Cider Cellar. Thackeray describes it thus:

"Healthy country tradesmen and farmers in London for their business, came and recreated themselves with the jolly singing and suppers at the Back Kitchen; squads of young apprentices and assistants — the shutters being closed over the scene of their labours — came hither, for fresh air doubtless. Dashing young medical students, gallant, clashing, what is called loudly dressed and must it be owned? somewhat dirty, came here, smoking and drinking and vigorously applauding the songs; young University bucks were to be found here, too, with that indescribable simper which is only learned at the knees of Alma Mater, and handsome young guardsmen and florid bucks from the St James' Street clubs." According to one authority here came, in their early days, Louis Napolean and Benjamin Disraeli. *(Illustration 92)*

Voltaire, exiled to England in 1725, lived on the

89. *J. M. W. Turner, by George Dance, 1800.*

south side too, in 1727-8, at a hairdressers called the White Peruke. Its location is not known and it is conceivable that it could have been a hairdressers preceding William Turner's period at No 21. Not too much inference can be drawn from this coincidence as continuity of trade in one building was not as common then as in the later part of that century. Voltaire returned to Paris in 1729.

Andrew Marvell, the poet and politician, stayed at No 9 in 1677 while an impoverished MP for Hull. His political fortunes survived the Restoration and he served in Parliament for 22 years. It is recorded that while in Maiden Lane he received a visit from an emissary of Charles II who offered him some money — no doubt a kindly gift from the King to help ease Marvell's poverty. Assuming the offer to be a bribe, Marvell haughtily refused it and carried on dining from the remains of a mutton bone. He died the following year. *(Illustration 90)*

90. *Andrew Marvell.*

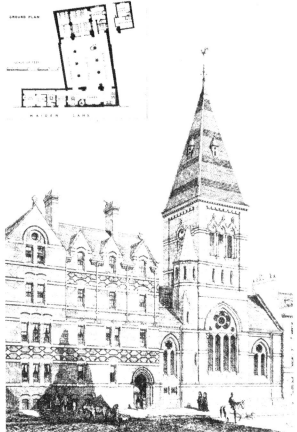

91. *Corpus Christi Church, Maiden Lane. From the Building News, 23rd October, 1874.*

A letter addressed to him here, shows that William Sancroft, later to become Archbishop of Canterbury, lived in Maiden Lane (location unknown) in 1663, when he was Dean of York. He became Dean of St Paul's Cathedral the following year and helped to supervise its rebuilding after the Great Fire of London. In 1677 he was made Archbishop of Canterbury but when, in 1687, he drew up a petition against the reading of the Declaration of Indulgence, he was imprisoned in the Tower with six other bishops. He was later acquitted. More trouble came later when he refused to take the Oath of Allegiance to William and Mary and was suspended.

South Side
Corpus Christi Roman Catholic Church

This was built in 1874 to the designs of Frederick Hyde Pownall. It has simple and unremarkable architecture inside and out. It was built on the site of some houses and a pub. (*Illustration 91*)

Vaudeville Theatre Nos 9/10

The rear of this theatre, built in 1870, displays a handsome fan-like casing above the first floor window.

Nos 13/14

The Peacock stands on the site of premises which have been licensed since at least 1690.

Nos 16/17

These buildings now look rather dreary with their 19th century frontage, but they were built c1807. No 16 was a dairy for nearly a hundred years.

North Side
No 27

This was used briefly as a parochial school for girls in the 1860s, and then became a military outfitters for at least forty years. It is still remembered as housing a very good herbalist from the 1920s to 1970, an offshoot of an old-established market business whose name is still

92. The Cider Cellar, No 21 Maiden Lane.

engraved on the west front of the central market building.

No 29

This building is actually the rear entrance to 15/16 Henrietta Street, built in 1888. At the turn of this century it was used, as was the front, for a Poor Relief Office, then Registry Office. It is now converted into studios.

No 31

This is the rear entrance to the old Ashley's Hotel in Henrietta Street, built in 1879. In the 1920s it was used as offices by Spicers, the paper-makers, and then in the 1930s by Henry Booth (Hull) Ltd, specialists in ticket printing.

Nos 34/35

This is Rules, one of the oldest established restaurants in London. Benjamin Rule, fish-monger, originally had premises at Nos 36 and 38 back to 1828, as far as can be established, although the restaurant assert that the business began in 1798. In 1873, No 35 was built — there the oyster bar was established. No 34 was built in 1876 and until the 1960s was used by a chemical apparatus manufacturer until Rules extended their premises. The food and interior are both

93. Nos 26/27 Maiden Lane, one of the two homes in this street of J. M. W. Turner.

94. *Rules Restaurant, Maiden Lane.*

very good. On the first floor is a curtained alcove in which Edward VII entertained his mistress Lily Langtry, the actress, their coming and going being carefully managed by a discreet use of staircases. Dickens and Thackeray were regular diners here. *(Illustration 94)*

Nos 36-39

Sussex Mansions, an Edwardian block, is on the site of the original premises of Benjamin Rule, fishmonger (See Nos 34/35).

No 41

Henri's Bedford Head was originally The Bedford Head, established on this site in 1747.

MART STREET

This street was formed in 1932-3 when the old Tavistock Hotel was demolished. It was one of the few developments commissioned by the Covent Garden Properties Co Ltd, owned by Sir Thomas Beecham and his brother.

MARTLETT COURT

This passageway goes between blocks and has no houses; originally it did not open into Drury Lane.

The only interesting snippet of information about it is contained in *'The Annals of Covent Garden'* where, we are told (although the author doesn't know for sure), that Harriet Mellon, the actress, used to entertain her benefactor Thomas Coutts, the wealthy banker, here. This lady had a spectacular career. Aided by the generosity of Coutts, she took a lease on a large house, Holly Lodge, in Highgate and married him when his wife died in 1815 — he was 80 and she 38. Coutts died seven years later and she then married, in 1827, her neighbour the 9th Duke of St Albans. She had inherited the Coutts money, which was very substantial, and when she died she left the fortune to Thomas Coutts' grand-daughter, later to become the famous Baroness Burdett-Coutts.

MAYS COURT

This 17th century passageway between Bedfordbury and St Martin's Lane is now rebuilt with new buildings on its north side and the flank wall of the Coliseum Theatre on its south. Originally called Mays Buildings, it carried on across Bedfordbury through to Bedford Court, where there was then access to Bedford Street. This part officially disappeared when Bedford Court was realigned to come through to Bedfordbury.

The Court is named after a builder who rebuilt it in 1739. His own house here lasted until at least 1920.

MERCER STREET

Mercer Street is partly derelict, especially at the Seven Dials end. As its name implies it is on land owned by the Mercers' Company and quite a few of the buildings here carry the Mercers' insignia — a saintly lady, which may perhaps have been a saintly boy originally — within a cartouche. Maidstone and Tonbridge Houses and Chertsey Chambers were built by the Mercers' Company in the 1920s — very handsomely as artisans' dwellings go, faced with brown tiles and imposing pediments.

Macready's Club, on the corner with Shelton Street, is for theatre people who like to stop work and talk about it. It used to be the Mercers' Arms, (the name is still there high up). Macready was an actor in the first half of the 19th century.

95. Neal Street c1900.

NEAL STREET

About 1700 Sir Thomas Neale, Master of the Mint, was responsible for laying out the streets radiating from Seven Dials. His commemoration in this street name is relatively new (1870s), the thoroughfare being called King Street back to the 17th century. The name was changed because of its confusing nearness to King Street, off Covent Garden Market.

Some of the street has been demolished and the rest is mainly 19th century industrial building. Nos 27-37 are older and so, probably, is No 33, No 69 is early 19th century and now specialises in selling kites. *(Illustration 95)*

West Side

No 33

This is one of the premises of Ellen Keeley, a firm specialising in the manufacture of market barrows. Other premises are in Nottingham Court and in Shorts Gardens where flowers are sold. The Keeley and O'Doherty families came to England at the time of the potato famine in Ireland and made their homes in Nottingham Court. In time they were united by marriage. James Keeley, meanwhile, invented and produced the costermonger's barrow, the one that we all see today, like a shop on wheels. He developed also the donkey barrow, which was a common feature in London until the last War. The business is still retained in the O'Doherty family, the head of

96. No 33 Neal Street in 1968.

97. No 33 Neal Street in 1911.

which has a collection of barrows, coaches and carriages at his farm in Hertfordshire. (See illustrations 96 and 97 for comparisons of their Neal Street premises spanning nearly 60 years.)

East Side
No 78
This property is now divided into two shops, but you can still see the facade of the Fountain pub which closed its doors in the 1930s.

No 68
At the side of this building is an entrance leading to a storehouse at the rear, which used to be a small chapel (a listed building).

Nos 26/32
The occupiers of these 19th century market warehouses have done their best to make us look up to see how well they have renovated and decorated them. All to no avail, probably, because one is tempted to gaze hungrily in to No 26 at the

Neal Street Restaurant, wondering if the inner man or woman should have a treat.

No 24
The Crown and Anchor pub was rebuilt in 1904 but there was an inn of that name here in 1800 and probably before that.

NEALS YARD
This impressive courtyard of warehouses is between Shorts Gardens and Monmouth Street. It is being lovingly restored. In particular the Wholefood Warehouse gets top marks for its flower display on hoist platforms and the modern dovecote (really a pigeoncote). Don't walk underneath but do stop and stare.

In this Yard are premises of Robert White & Sons, armourers, who have been here for nearly 200 years.

NEW ROW

Until the 1860s New Row was a much used way from King Street into St Martin's Lane and it must have become very congested with market traffic. Then Garrick Street was opened and New Row (called New Street until 1937) became a much quieter small-shop thoroughfare. Nowadays it ranks as a candidate for paving over.

Building commenced in 1635 and it was finished by 1644; it replaced Castle and Sunne Alleys. It probably contained some substantial houses at this time. The Countess of Chesterfield and, later, Lady Stanhope, lived in one on the site of the White Swan. Some c1700 houses remain and good shop fronts, notably at Nos 16/18,

survive. Others, like No 6, have been vulgarised. No 19, which used to be the Green Man pub was, together with No 20, extensively altered earlier this century.

Dr Johnson, who must have known virtually every tavern and eating house in Covent Garden, is recorded as having been frequently to the Pine Apple here, but its location is unknown.

John Flaxman (1755-1826), the sculptor, lived here in his younger days at his father's plaster shop. From here he sent his first contribution, a modelled head, to the Royal Academy. *(Illustration 99).*

98. No 21 New Row in 1903.

Nos 4, 5, 6 and 9
All these buildings date from c1700 and perhaps even before.

No 13
This has a very attractive shop-front, looking quite venerable — however, it is fairly new. Until quite recently it had been occupied by a bakers for at least a hundred years.

No 14
The White Swan is built on the site of a house which the Countess of Chesterfield (1658-63) and Lady Stanhope (1664-7) occupied. It has beautifully decorated stone work outside, but the interior is disappointing.

Nos 16/18
Some attempt has been made to restore this group of 18th century buildings. No 16, with its slate mansard roof, is the best looking, retaining its lion motif at the top of its exterior pillars.

Nos 21/22
The ground floor of these premises has been re-

99. New Row, looking south, in 1966.

built to blend sensitively with the street. The present occupiers, Thomas Bland, gun-makers, have made the most of their building. They were established in 1840 but are newcomers to New Row. The previous occupants, Littlewood Brothers, had been here for at least sixty years, selling hardware — they have, or had, a number of shops in the Covent Garden area. Before that butchers were in business. *(Illustration 98)*

NEWTON STREET
The northern part of Newton Street, down to Macklin Street, was so named in the 17th century after William Newton, a speculative builder who also designed Lincolns Inn Fields. The southern half of the present street, called Cross Lane, terminated at Parker Street, and the present, grudging continuation through the bowels of an office block into Great Queen Street, reflects this earlier street pattern. Like a number of streets in this area, it is dominated by what were called 'Artisans Dwellings', to replace the awful slums that were there. In 1913 both the *Pall Mall Gazette* and the *Observer* were published in the southern half of the street.

NOTTINGHAM COURT
This has no architectural interest and is scheduled to be rebuilt on its west side for housing. At one end is the London Medical Mission. On the west, usually identifiable from the barrows outside, is one of the premises of the firm called Ellen Keeley (See 33 Neal Street for a description of this business).

On the east, W.T. Morrell & Co Ltd, bookbinders, have been here for about 65 years, having been founded in Soho in 1861. There are not many craft bookbinders left in London — Sangorski and Sutcliffe in Poland Street is another — where individual books can be bound and embellished.

The Court was built c1710 and named after Daniel Finch, 2nd Earl of Nottingham, a leading politician in the reign of Queen Anne, who lived in St Giles-in-the-Fields.

OLD BREWERS' YARD
This Yard is situated between Nos 32 and 34 Shelton Street. The last brewers occupying these premises were Watney Combe, but it is likely that

they were not the first such company to be here. The buildings are gradually being converted, like so many in the area, into studios and workshops.

In the 18th century, when it was formed, it was called Wood's Yard.

PARKER STREET

In the St Giles-in-the-Fields 'Rookeries' area in 1839, the density of people to the acre, as planners call it, was 2522. In, say, West Kentish Town, one of Camden's most crowded areas, the density now is 200 per acre. One cannot be too certain of the higher figure but it gives an indication of the squalid conditions people endured. Parker Street, formerly Parkers Lane (built 1615 and named after Philip Parker, a local landowner), would have been part of this appalling overcrowding. Its domination today by charity dwellings reflects the determination of the late 19th century reformers to improve the conditions of the poor. Unfortunately, the architecture is rather depressing.

Nos 34/38 is a distinguished building, formerly

Parker Street · Drury Lane

100. Parker Street in the 18th century.

the business of an auctioneers and then of Philips Electrical.

It is worth going to the Kingsway end of the street just to see the florid stone figures supporting bay windows on the side of Nos 105/7 Kingsway. The Kingsway Tavern on the other side, is on the site of a much older pub called the Crown and Cushion. *(Illustration 100)*

ROSE STREET

Before the 1860s Rose Street used to be one complete dog-leg shape. At that time Floral Street was extended west into Garrick Street, then being built, separating Rose Street into two parts. It is known particularly well, despite its obscurity and narrowness, because it houses the Lamb and Flag pub. There is an interesting vista, in its northern part, of 18th century houses, some spoilt by modern doors, and a three storey warehouse over the archway. Otherwise, the street is mainly the backs and sides of buildings of other streets — notably the rear of the old Westminster Fire Office.

Rose Street had a particularly bad reputation both for its immorality and its insanitary conditions. As originally built in the 1630s, the houses were "fitt for mechaniks only and persons of meane quallite'. It was the scene, in 1679, of an attack on the poet Dryden, when he was set upon by three men and beaten. It is said that they were paid to do so by the Earl of Rochester as a reprisal for a satire on him he thought had been written by Dryden, but was actually written by someone else. Dryden offered fifty pounds reward for the discovery of the attackers and their instigator but it was never claimed.

The Street's most famous resident was Samuel Butler (1612-80) the author of *Hudibras*, a book which satirised the Puritans. He died here in poverty, which only goes to show that there is more money to be made in writing about the rich than the abstemious. *(Illustration 101)*

The Lamb and Flag

On the ceiling of the passageway, Lazenby Court, which leads through the side of the pub, the proprietors have displayed in suitably Olde English lettering, a notice which reads:

'Stay traveller rest and refresh yrself in this

101. Samuel Butler, drawn by T. Uwins.

102. The Lamb and Flag, Rose Street, 1968.

ancient tavern in whose walls so many great figures of the past have taken their ease. Here often sat the immortal Charles Dickens & his friends, poor Samuel Butler and the wits and gallants of the restoration. Hither resorted the Bucks and Dandies to witness prize fights & cock mains, while hard by was enacted the notorious Rose Alley Ambuscade in Decr 1679 when the poet Dryden was almost done to death at the instance of Louise de Keroualle, mistress of Charles II'.

The attack, you will note, has a different instigator than the one mentioned earlier. To compound this, Professor Pinto in his book *Enthusiast in Wit,* suggests that the attack was engineered by the Earl of Pembroke.

Unfortunately for the rest of the inscription the best-researched books are inclined to spoil a good story, as is the case here. The *Survey of London Volume 36* is quite sure that though a building existed on this site by 1639, this particular structure is early 18th century, which does rule out poor Butler being there, amongst others. Furthermore, and here the Survey is not quite so adamant, the Lamb and Flag (only called such since 1833) was not in this building until 1772. The Lamb and Flag was previously called the Coopers Arms and in the 18th century there was, on the other side of the alley, an inn of that name, the inference being that the inn moved premises in 1772. So, on this assumption, the wits and gallants of the Restoration were sitting with their tankards in another building probably looking out at the one that was here before this one.

The pub was refaced with bricks in 1958 but looks authentically old — the bricklayer's name deserves a credit somewhere.

The interior of the Lamb and Flag, if you can see it through the mass of people, is simple and attractive and an 18th century staircase leads you to the upper room, sometimes used as a theatre. The Lamb and Flag are featured in the arms of the Middle Temple. *(Illustration 102)*

Lazenby Court was formed in 1688 when the second building on this site was erected.

RUSSELL STREET

Before the market buildings were erected in the square in 1830, Russell Street would have had the best vista in the Covent Garden scheme. The Church faced it and the Piazza buildings would have come gradually into view as the Square was approached. The compensation now is that once renovation of the market is finished and the hoardings come down, Russell Street will once again have an enviable view.

The heyday of the street was in the coffee-house era. Three of the best known — Tom's, Button's and Will's — vied for custom. (Will's on the corner of Russell and Bow Streets, is dealt with under Bow Street). And at No 8 took place a meeting that was to lead to one of the classics of British literature — James Boswell was introduced to Dr Johnson.

Other famous names associated with Russell Street are John Evelyn, the diarist, who took rooms here in 1659/60, and Charles Lamb and his sister Mary, who lodged at No 20 in 1817. Charles Lamb wrote to Dorothy Wordsworth about it: 'The theatres with all their noises, Covent Garden, dearer to me than any gardens of Alcinous, where we are morally sure of the earliest peas and 'sparagus; Bow Street, where the thieves are examined, within a few yards of us. Mary had not been here four and twenty hours before she saw a Thief. She sits at the window working, and casually throwing out her eyes, she sees a concourse of people coming this way, with a constable to conduct the solemnity'.

The original William Hickey (1749-1830), journalist, records an evening at one of the more disreputable houses in the street, almost certainly at the eastern end. At the door Hickey and his friends were scrutinised by a 'cut throat looking rascal' peering through a small wicket. They were admitted one by one. The first titillation offered them was that of two half-naked, bleeding and wholly drunken women having a wrestling match. Later 'an uncommonly athletic young man of about twenty-five' was introduced whose role was to be attacked by 'no less than three Amazonian tigresses with sticks. The central figure retaliated to the best of his considerable ability, knocking each assailant down with his fists whenever opportunity offered.' *(Illustrations 103 and 108)*

103. *Tom's Coffee House, 16/17 Russell Street.*

North side
Nos 13/15 (now the vacant corner with the square)

No buildings exist here now where once stood some arcaded houses and the Old Red Lion pub. Instead we have a hard-won garden decorated in nice humour with lions supporting a slab seat and some ruined terrace pillars, for all the world as though some adjacent country house had fallen into disuse and disrepair.

No 17

This building is now partly used. In the early 18th century it was Tom's Coffee House, used mainly by the theatrical profession and not to be confused with two other establishments bearing the same name outside of Covent Garden. This one was founded by Captain Thomas West in

1700. In 1722, apparently driven to extreme by gout, he threw himself to his death from a second floor window at the back. Before the coffee-house John Evelyn, the diarist, lodged at a house on this site in 1659.

Nos 19/20

These both retain attractive shop fronts despite their long use by market traders. The Brahms and Liszt restaurant occupies No 19 which was, in the early part of the 19th century, a coffee-house.

Telephone Exchange

This was erected in 1927, designed by J.H. Markham. Its most prominent feature is the way the windows project at third floor level. A recent extension to this old Temple Bar Exchange (those of us whose initial geography of London was built upon telephone exchange names will remember this one), is in Bow Street.

Fortune Theatre

For a theatre, it has an undistinguished exterior. It was built in 1924, the first new theatre erected in London after the 1st World War. A passageway — the entrance to the Scottish Church to the rear — runs the whole length of the theatre at the side.

Drury House

This flamboyant building is now the auction rooms of Stanley Gibbons, the stamp dealers — a reminder of the concentration of philatelists in the Strand area.

South Side
Nos 1/4

These buildings, now being renovated, were built in 1776.

No 8

It was here in the back parlour (now demolished) of this 1760 house, that the famous meeting between James Boswell and Dr Johnson took place. Boswell describes it thus:

'Mr Davies, the actor, who then kept a bookseller's shop in Russell Street, Covent Garden, told me that Johnson was very much his friend, and came frequently to his house, where he more than once invited me to meet him; but by some unlucky accident or other he was prevented from coming to us.

At last, on Monday, the 16th of May (in 1763), when I was sitting in Mr Davies's back parlour,

104. *James Boswell.*

105. *Dr. Johnson, from a painting by Sir Joshua Reynolds.*

106. No 8 Russell Street, from a watercolour.

107. No 8 Russell Street in 1942.

after having drunk tea with him and Mrs Davies, Johnson unexpectedly came into the shop; and Mr Davies having perceived him, through the glass-door in the room in which we were sitting, advancing towards us, he announced his awful approach to me, somewhat in the manner of an actor in the part of Horatio, when he addresses Hamlet on the appearance of his father's ghost, "Look, my lord, it comes!"

Davies, knowing Johnson's aversion to Scotsmen, mischievously told Johnson that Boswell was Scots and Boswell in some embarrassment said "I do indeed come from Scotland, but I cannot help it." "That Sir" replied Johnson, "I find, is what a very great many of your countrymen cannot help."

The house is listed as Grade II and is at the moment being renovated and converted by the GLC; it will become 'an 18th century coffeehouse'. *(Illustrations 104, 105, 106 and 107)*

No 9

The Market House pub, plain outside and in, was until the beginning of this century, the Northumberland Arms. There has been a pub on this site since at least 1708.

No 10

A hairdressers has recently opened here on the site of what used to be Button's Coffee House (opened 1712). Button himself had previously been a servant to Lady Warwick who took, as her second husband, Addison of *Spectator* fame. It was Addison who set Button up in business and patronized it together with Pope, Swift, Steele and Colley Cibber. In this establishment was a free-standing letterbox called the Lion's Head (such was its form), into which contributors to the *Guardian* newspaper — not the present-day one, but an Addison publication described later as High Church and Gladstonian — placed their offerings of news, scandal and tit-bits.

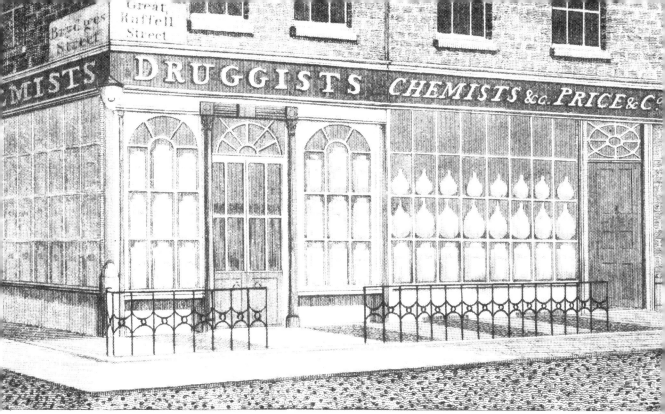

108. Price and Co, Russell Street, early 19th century.

SHELTON STREET

Shelton Street, now mainly 19th century ware-housing, is on the line of the 17th century Castle Street. The old street terminated at the east at Dirty Lane (now Arne Street) and then continued via Turnstile Alley into Drury Lane. That alley is represented today by the very narrow part of Shelton Street at its eastern end.

William Shelton was a vestryman of St Giles, who bequeathed money in 1672 to clothe 20 aged parish paupers each year and provide education for 50 poor children. The street was named after him in 1877.

In the early part of the 19th century, almost all the business premises here housed carpenters and furniture shops. Here too was an ironmongery shop called Huxley and Heriot which, in 1863, had become the premises of Comyn Ching. It is sad that these modest buildings are not to be restored, due to cost.

On the south side between Arne Street and Endell Street (now being redeveloped) stood, in the late 19th century, the St Martin's National Schools. They were joined later by the St Martin's District School of Art, forerunner of the well-known art school in Charing Cross Road, who are now taking extra premises in Long Acre. Other semi-public buildings on this side were the Artisans' Institute for Promoting General and Technical Education and the Hanover House Home for Working Boys in London, both swept away to provide warehousing for the market.

On the north side is the Earlham Street Ware-house, which is owned by the GLC and houses the enterprising Covent Garden Community Centre. Outside, in traditional style, is a very attractive hanging 'trade sign'. It is proposed to convert the fifth floor of this building for resid-ential purposes and to add a new sixth floor over much of the building.

SHORTS GARDENS

This evocative name is dampened by a generally run-down, architecturally undistinguished street. William Short of Grays Inn cultivated a garden here in the late 16th century; his family later built a house in the area.

The road originally ran from Drury Lane to Neal Street only, but when Seven Dials was constructed in the last decade of the 17th century, it was extended westward to become one of the seven roads radiating from the central column.

There are few entries in the 19th century directories for this street which indicates either that the class of trade was so poor as not to warrant notice, or else that it was residential. The former is the more likely.

The eastern end from Endell Street to Drury Lane is dreary, saved only by the very attractive side of St Paul's Hospital which fronts Endell Street. The windows have very striking mouldings surrounding them.

The next stretch between Endell Street and Neal Street contains, on the north side, the headquarters (Nos 43/45) of the Covent Garden Community Association, which is the 'political' wing of the local residents, pouring out a great deal of literature, which seeks to remedy what they claim are the errors of councils, planners, commercial interests and valuers. Opposite them is Nottingham House, a recently modernised, but still depressing, block erected by the Society for Improving the Condition of the Labouring Classes.

The remaining, western, section has the most interesting buildings. No 22 on the south is very self-assured mid Victorian and well preserved — on the outside anyway. Nos 4 and 6 are of the same period, No 6 selling an overwhelming range of oriental goods, and No 4 houses Ellen Keeley, florist, the business having been here for at least 45 years. (See Neal Street for details of the Keeley firm). It has its own clock outside.

On the opposite north side Nos 23/25 are the premises of Newmans the chocolate manufacturers. Anchel Newman, an American, arrived from Australia in 1927 and set up shop in the area; his son now manages the business. If you like chocolates, try these. They are original, blended from secret recipes, and a far cry from the run-of-the-mill English variety. Newmans have four shops in central London.

SLINGSBY PLACE

This now appears to be a private courtyard, off Long Acre. It is named after Sir William Slingsby, a 17th century landowner. On the face of one of the 19th century buildings can still be seen an advertisement for motor body builders

and repairs, evidence of this area's concentration on first, coachbuilding, and then motor cars.

SMARTS PLACE

Virtually the whole of this street has been demolished and almost all the rest consists of the sides of other buildings. Miss Bebbington in her *London Street Names*, tells us that William Smart, a carpenter, lived here in 1710 — there is an unnamed roadway on the same site on the 1660s map, but the 1746 Rocque map calls it Cole Yard, a name also given to Stukeley Street.

It has been suggested that Cole Yard derived its name from the storage of coal here, but as a 'Bassit Cole Esq' lived nearby in 1646 it is probable that it was named after him.

The St Giles and St George's Almshouses were at Nos 9/10 from 1783 to the 1960s. Part of their premises included the old Round House, an early prison.

If one of several stories can be accepted, Nell Gwyn was born here. Her father, Thomas, put a 'Captain' before his name and claimed descent from an ancient Welsh family, but other accounts say that he was a fruiterer. In any case the family was poor and Nell at an early age was selling fruit

109. Nell Gwyn.

in Covent Garden before becoming an actress and the King's mistress — a rags-to-riches story with hardly a parallel in this country. One of the many places where she did sleep, as opposed to those where it is *said* that she slept, is Lauderdale House in Highgate, now being renovated. She died in 1687, aged 38, and was buried in St. Martin's-in-the-Fields churchyard. An American was, some years back, trying to prove that her remains had been reinterred in St. Martin's graveyard in Camden Town in the 19th century. *(Illustration 109)*

SOUTHAMPTON STREET

Southampton Street is built on the grounds of Bedford House — demolished in 1706. Only two of the original houses, Nos 26 and 27, survive. Market activities, although so near, were not allowed to intrude on the street and until 1872 there was a bar across to prohibit market traffic.

Its residents have included David Garrick (see No 27), and Dr Lempriére, author of the famous *Classical Dictionary* who died here in 1824. W. S. Gilbert of Gilbert and Sullivan fame, was born here in 1836, reputedly at No 17 (now demolished), and Colley Cibber, the actor, lodged here 1714-20. Boswell tells us that he lost his virginity at a house in this street to one, Sally Forrester, in 1762.

East Side
No 3

At this address was printed William Cobbett's daily newspaper *The Porcupine* in 1800, a journal so prickly that it was attacked by a mob in 1801 for its political opinions. The present Post Office building was built c1904. The baroque clock outside was designed by Edward Lutyens for George Newnes, the publishers, who had offices above. Originally the clock face spelled out the name George Newnes instead of having numerals.

Nos 8/14 Tower House

This is one of the buildings once occupied by George Newnes, publishers of popular magazines. Sir George Newnes (1851-1910), was born in Matlock and was one of the first, together with C. Arthur Pearson in Henrietta Street, to exploit the new literacy of the age. His success was based upon *Tit-Bits*, first published in 1881 and still going, and his other titles included *Ladies Field,*

110. *Garrick House, 27 Southampton Street.*

Strand, *Woman's Life* and *John O'London's Weekly.* Today Newnes is owned by the International Printing Corporation.

West side
Nos 22-25

The Lloyds Bank building was erected in 1878 as the Covent Garden Hotel, which lasted until the 1920s. By 1923 Sherrys Restaurant was at No 25, to be replaced in the 1930s by the Boulestin Restaurant which is still there.

No 26

This was erected in 1708, its first occupant being a lawyer, but thereafter it was a private residence until 1746, when it reverted to business use. In 1823 the London Gaslight Company was here, in 1903 a doctor, and in 1913 Samuel French, theatrical publishers. In the late 1960s this firm extended their premises to include No 27, although they have just vacated the latter.

The firm of Samuel French began in 1830, when 20-year-old Thomas Lacy set up shop at 27 Wellington Street selling acting editions of plays. His business just preceded the lifting of the performing monopoly of Covent Garden and

111. Nos 30/31 Southampton Street in 1893 (now demolished).

Drury Lane theatres and soon there were more theatres than printed plays to go round. Samuel French had, at roughly the same time, begun a similar business in America and Lacy and he exchanged scripts across the Atlantic. In 1872, French settled in England and bought out Lacy, developing the business until his death in 1898.

No 27 Garrick House

This house was the residence of the actor David Garrick from 1749-1772, although the plaque outside says that he was here from 1750 onwards. Garrick (born 1717), was educated at Lichfield, partly under the tuition of Dr Johnson with whom he came to London in 1737. One of Garrick's specialities was a cruel impersonation of Mrs Johnson. First, Garrick went into the wine trade with his brother, but became an actor in 1741. His ideas on how to produce Shakespeare were controversial at the time. He reverted to the original scripts, dressed his actors in costumes appropriate to a play's period and setting, and prevented his audiences from sitting on the stage. Some of these innovations are quite often over-

112. David Garrick as Tancred, by Thomas Worlidge.

turned nowadays. From him came, during his term as part-proprietor of Drury Lane Theatre, the theatrical world 'props' or 'properties': each of the costumes he had made was labelled with the words 'The Property of the Management'. A ballet production of his in 1755 produced such a response from the audience that some members smashed the windows of his house.

Garrick Street and the Garrick Club there, are named after him.

The interior of the house has the original staircase — very creaky — and much of its old panelling on the ground floor. In the basement is a lead water tank dated 1713. It is apt that the house should be used until recently by Samuel French, the theatrical publisher, and in the 1970s by the Greater London Arts Association. *(Illustrations 110 and 111)*

After Garrick came a lawyer and then in 1801, Easteys Family Hotel until 1863. Another theatrical tenant, in 1948, was Peter Daubeney, the impressario.

Nos 34-38

These buildings have a green and blue tiled fascia. They were erected in 1896, the tenants being publishers called Weldon.

Previously, at No 36 — a reminder of old battles won but not necessarily over — was the Campaign for the Abolition of Capital Punishment, in 1865-6.

STUKELEY STREET

Dr Stukeley (1687-1765), remembered chiefly as being an over-imaginative archaeologist, deserves better than to have his name given to this dispiriting back way. He lived in Great Ormond Street and was Rector of St. George's, Queen Square.

The only building to note, just because it is there, is the City Literary Institute, rebuilt in 1938.

Stukeley Street was originally called Cole Yard (see Smarts Place) and then Goldsmith Street.

TAVISTOCK STREET

Tavistock Street was built in three parts. The central section, running from Wellington Street to Catherine Street, came first in the 4th Earl of Bedford's Covent Garden scheme in the 1630s. It was then called York Street. When Bedford House was demolished in 1706 Tavistock Street was then constructed between Southampton Street and York Street. In 1900 an extension to the old York Street was made, east to Drury Lane across the old St Mary-le-Strand burial ground. The three parts were renamed and renumbered Tavistock Street in 1937, the name deriving from a Bedford family seat.

In the 18th and early 19th centuries the street was particularly known for its booksellers and publishers. At Nos 34/36 were Henry Bohn, well-known in the book trade of the day from 1835-66. Where the roadway crosses Wellington Street is the site of a bookselling business owned by Samuel Baker from 1753; he established here the first saleroom to deal only with books, manuscripts and prints. When he died the business passed to his nephew John Sotheby — from this shop developed Sotheby's the auctioneers. *(Illustration 116)*

Various magazines were published here. The 1883 directory shows *The World* at what is now 42, *The British Journal of Photography* at 40, *The Statist* at 38, *The Whitehall Review* at 34, *The Insurance Record* at 15 and *Bicycling News* at 17. The best-known magazines to have residence here have been *Vanity Fair* and *The Lady* at roughly where No 20 is, *The Stage* at 19/21, and *Country Life* at No 2.

113. Nos 34-38 Tavistock Street in 1958.

Nos 2/10

This building, now empty and being converted, was designed by Sir Edwin Lutyens in 1905 in what has been called his "Wrenaissance' style. It housed the magazine *Country Life*, that seemingly permanent part of our inheritance. It was founded in 1897 by Edward Hudson, proprietor of a printing company in Southwark, in association with George Newnes. Oddly, Mr. Hudson's original printing company, known later as Keliher, Hudson and Kearns became, after some changes of ownership, part of the British Printing Corporation which now prints *Country Life* through its subsidiary Waterlows.

Hudson was well-known in the area for the way in which he crossed the Strand for lunch each day, imperiously holding up the traffic with his arm upraised. He owned a high-roofed Rolls-Royce, with folding steps on the running board and two exhausts on the bonnet.

The building doesn't really have enough room to appear too distinguished but Lutyens spent a long time designing it — his first major building in London.

Nos 34/38

This is a very satisfying group of houses built in 1733. Do not be misled by an old plaque set high up on Nos 34/36 which bears the words 'Yorke Street 1636'. York Street is the former name of this section of the street and the plaque, no doubt, was rescued when the original houses were demolished.

In 1821, Thomas de Quincey (1785-1859) lodged in a room behind No 36 and here wrote *'The Confessions of an English Opium Eater'*, his first major work. Indulgence in opium was then a curiosity rather than a reason for a dawn raid and there was considerable discussion as to whether it increased longevity or not. De Quincey (he added the 'De') was never able to break his reliance on it. He moved to Scotland in 1830 and lived there till he died, moving from lodging to lodging. At his death he was paying rent on six separate abodes.

The restaurant at No 36 is named after him. *(Illustration 113)*

North Side
No 11 (with 28 Wellington Street)

Substantially, this is a 1752 building with a fairly modern and attractive paned shop front. It has been, for most of its existence, a wine merchant, then a wholesale florist.

No 13

These premises are occupied by Littlewood Brothers, a hardware firm with branches in other parts of London, including, until recently, one in New Row. They have been here since the beginning of this century.

No 15

The shop front of this 1729 building has been unmercifully vulgarised. It was erected by a carpenter and that trade was still carried on here in the 1860s. The *Insurance Record* was here in the 1880s and the *Spectator* in the 1920s.

Nos 17/19

The former offices of *The Stage* were erected in 1753. No 17 has also housed the *Horse and Hound* magazine at the turn of this century, which is about the date *The Stage* came here.

WELLINGTON STREET

In the 4th Earl of Bedford's scheme for Covent Garden in the 1630s one part of Wellington Street was built. It ran from Russell Street down to what was later Tavistock Street, and he called it Charles Street. The road was extended to the Strand and there met its Waterloo Bridge in 1835 — this was after the English Opera House, which stood across the present line of the road, had burnt down. The whole thoroughfare was later renamed after the Iron Duke. *(Illustration 115)*

West side
The Lyceum Theatre

The Lyceum stands on part of ground once occupied by Cecil (or Exeter) House. A building used for various entertainments was here in 1765, and in c1790 a playhouse began, only to have its licence withdrawn after pressure from the Covent Garden and Drury Lane theatres. After a phase of short-lived enterprises it was opened in 1809 as the English Opera House. When this proved successful it was rebuilt in 1816, only to follow the fate of the other two theatres and be destroyed by fire in 1830.

In 1831 a new building arose on this slightly different site and it entered into its golden age, with Henry Irving and Ellen Terry the stars. It

114. *The Lyceum.*

was the first theatre in London to have gas lighting on the stage. *(Illustrations 114 and 116)*

It is a dance-hall now, full of the ghosts of young people who began relationships on the dance floor, timing their persuasive conversation to the old routine of three tunes per rhythm, before the orchestra stopped and it became necessary in the silence thereafter to take the conversation further or merely to say "thank you".

Of the 1831 building just about only the portico survives. The architect was Samuel Beazley.

No 21

It is a pity that this mid Victorian building in yellow and red brick is in such bad repair, because it could ornament the corner into Exeter Street. Since the 1860s it has been a wine merchant, a papier mâché factory, a wholesale florist and for at least forty years, a café.

No 23

The Old Bell Tavern, rebuilt in 1835, has a good wooden frontage. The upper storeys have lost three windows because of the Window Tax, but an old gas lamp remains. The inaugural meeting of the London Corresponding Society, a prominent political reform group, was convened here in 1792. Over the bar is a 1915 photograph showing the damage caused to the pub and No 21 by a nearby bomb.

Nos 25/31

This 1930s block has a place in newspaper history, being on the site of the first offices of the *Reynolds News*, founded by George McArthur Reynolds in the middle of the 19th century. It is described in a contemporary list as 'democratic in the lower classes'. It was, in fact, a left-wing newspaper, intent on reforming the electoral system to give the working-classes more say. It was eventually owned by the Co-operative movement, which later gave it the bland title of *Sunday Citizen* which is, and was, enough to kill off any publication.

No 41

Penhaligons, perfumers (by Royal Warrant to the Duke of Edinburgh), occupy this shop — the interior must be seen and sensed. Walter Penhaligon was the Court Barber at the end of Queen Victoria's reign. He was born in Penzance in 1841 and, coming to London as a young man, established himself as a barber in Jermyn Street. In the back of the shop he made exclusive perfumes, toilet waters and powders. Present day products are still made from recipes in his original notebooks. The business later went to Old Bond Street and came here to Wellington Street in 1975.

East Side
No 42

There has been a Coach and Horses pub here since at least 1753. The present building is c1860 and has a good decorated ceiling.

No 40

In 1726 the house on this site became the parsonage house of the parish of St Mary-le-Strand. The present building continued to be used so until 1876; there is still a plaque on the upper frontage with SMLS embossed. It came into market use c1910.

No 38

In the 18th century this was the Hanover Coffee House and very disorderly too. It must be pleasant to get disruptive just on coffee.

Nos 32/34

Crawford's Wine Bar used to be occupied by a wholesale florist. The new frontage has been sensitively introduced, reflecting both the needs

115. Sotheby's Auction Room in 1888 (see Tavistock Street).

of the business and the appearance of the street at this point.

No 26
Charles Dickens worked here. In 1850, he began a weekly newspaper at this address called *Household Words*, intended as a vehicle for new writers. This title was later changed to *All The Year Round*, which was still here in the 1880s.

No 18
The old headquarters of the Victoria Sporting Club is an ostentatious building designed by Charles Parnell in 1864. A stone horse's head survives above the entrance. The Club was formed in 1860 by a group of Blackfriars bookmakers and became a focus for professionals in the racing business, who came to hear the call-over of odds for races.

It stands on the site of C.F. Bielefeld's papier-mâché factory built in 1839 and, because of the fumes, a considerable nuisance in the area. Its

situation here was probably due to the nearby newspaper industry which used papier-mâché for making the moulds necessary for newspaper production.

WILD COURT
This court, which contains little of interest now, was probably built when Weld House was demolished in the 18th century. In the late 19th century, a number of the old hovels were renovated by the Society for Improving the Condition of the Labouring Classes. The Holy Trinity Mission was built at the same period.

WILD STREET
Weld House was erected by Humphrey Weld, son of an ex-Lord Mayor of London c1634. It was on the site of the late 19th century school on the east side, at present occupied by the City Literary Institute. At that time the house stood alone, but within twenty years the whole street had been built up.

116. Ellen Terry.

In the 19th century Wild Street, (the corruption to Wild began in the 17th century), was a street full of shops and small businesses on both sides. They included a swordsmith, four pubs, a phial manufacturer, ornamental painter and several premises allied to the carriage building trade centred on Long Acre.

Nowadays, four buildings take up most of the street: the side of the Freemasons' Hall (1927-33), Space House, a circular 1970s prefabricated tower block designed by Richard Seifert, part of the massive Peabody Estate which dominates the surrounding area (c1880), and a stolid Edwardian terra-cotta stucco and red-brick building once occupied by the Lambert and Butler tobacco firm. This latter building retains an ornate iron gateway with the firm's initials intertwined in its design. The company came here in the 1860s.

Further Reading

Survey of London, Vol 36, Parish of St Paul, Covent Garden (1970)

Survey of London, Vol 5, St Giles-in-the-Fields (part 2) (1914)

Survey of London, Vol 18, St Martin-in-the-Fields pt II (The Strand) (1937)

Survey of London, Vol 20, St Martin-in-the-Fields pt III (Trafalgar Square and Neighbourhood) (1940)

Names of Streets and Places in the Administrative County of London, LCC (1955)

The Buildings of England, London, Volume I, Nikolaus Pevsner (rev 1973)

London Street Names, Gillian Bebbington (1972)

Charles Dickens' London (1879)

A History of London Life, R. J. Mitchell and M. D. R. Leys, (1958)

Landlords to London, Simon Jenkins (1975)

A Social History of Housing 1815-1970, John Burnett (1978)

London Journal Vol 2 No 1 (1976) 'The Hunting Ground Beyond The Convent Garden'

The Companion Guide to London, David Piper, 6th edn (1977)

Covent Garden and Her Craftsmen, Marilyn Long (1975)

The Annals of Covent Garden and Its Neighbourhood, E. Beresford Chancellor (c1929)

From High Holborn to the Strand in Anno Domini MDCCCCIII, Henry Keen (1902)

My Covent Garden, Alan Dent (1973)

London Has a Garden, Clemence Dane (1964)

Covent Garden, Mary Cathcart Borer (1967)

Covent Garden's Moving, GLC (1968)

Covent Garden Action Area Plan, GLC (1978)

JS 100, The Story of Sainsburys (1969)

Viscount Southwood, R. J. Minney, (1954)

Oxford Companion to the Theatre, Hartnoll (1957)

The Bookman's London, Frank Swinnerton (1951)

The Theatres of London, Mander and Mitchenson (1955)

The Lost Theatres of London, Mander and Mitchenson (rev. 1976)

Theatre Royal, Drury Lane, W. Macqueen Pope (1945)

Drury Lane, Brian Dobbs (1972)

Index